T0113269

THE CARNAL MIND

Choosing to be Governed by the Spirit

ALYCE TALLMAN

WESTBOW
PRESS®
A DIVISION OF THOMAS NELSON
& ZONDERVAN

Copyright © 2016 Alyce Tallman.

All rights reserved. No part of this book may be used or reproduced by any means, graphic, electronic, or mechanical, including photocopying, recording, taping or by any information storage retrieval system without the written permission of the author except in the case of brief quotations embodied in critical articles and reviews.

Scripture taken from the New King James Version. Copyright © 1979, 1980, 1982 by Thomas Nelson, Inc. Used by permission. All rights reserved.

Scripture taken from the King James Version of the Bible.

Scripture taken from the *Amplified Bible*, copyright © 1954, 1958, 1962, 1964, 1965, 1987 by The Lockman Foundation. Used by permission.

WestBow Press books may be ordered through booksellers or by contacting:

WestBow Press
A Division of Thomas Nelson & Zondervan
1663 Liberty Drive
Bloomington, IN 47403
www.westbowpress.com
1 (866) 928-1240

Because of the dynamic nature of the Internet, any web addresses or links contained in this book may have changed since publication and may no longer be valid. The views expressed in this work are solely those of the author and do not necessarily reflect the views of the publisher, and the publisher hereby disclaims any responsibility for them.

Any people depicted in stock imagery provided by Thinkstock are models, and such images are being used for illustrative purposes only. Certain stock imagery © Thinkstock.

ISBN: 978-1-5127-3341-9 (sc)
ISBN: 978-1-5127-3342-6 (hc)
ISBN: 978-1-5127-3340-2 (e)

Library of Congress Control Number: 2016903432

Print information available on the last page.

WestBow Press rev. date: 4/6/2016

CONTENTS

DEDICATION

To my mom, whose strength and faith continue to amaze me;

To my husband and three daughters, who've been supportive and braved this faith-journey we've traveled together, much of which became book material;

And to my spiritual family, who has encouraged me with their confidence and conviction that this message be put in print.

Endorsements

"My wife, Joy, and I have worked closely with Alyce and Don Tallman for the past ten years. Pastor Alyce brings sound teaching and a high level of apostolic instruction in the Word that has greatly influenced me and many others in the Heartland. Through Topeka Storm Ministries, we co-labored together to bring regional revival events and establish a training center where she taught. I highly recommend this book to all with an 'ear to hear what the spirit is saying.'"

—Scott Logan, pastor, Tree of Life Fellowship,
and co-founder, Topeka Storm Ministries

"*The Carnal Mind* is an extremely well-researched discourse on the prevalent problem of 'mixing' the holy and the profane. Pastor Tallman has done a great job in outlining the problem of carnality in a Christian's life; but of even greater import, she provides a lot of scriptural keys on working with the Holy Spirit to subject the mind, will and emotions to His governing rule, thereby calling all Christians to come up higher in their walk of holiness before the Lord."

—Dr. James Maloney, author of *The Dancing Hand of God,*
The Panoramic Seer, Overwhelmed by the Spirit, The
Lord in the Fires, and *Living above the Snake Line*

FOREWORD

ooks like *The Carnal Mind* are confrontational. Once you've read them, they demand a response. Alyce Tallman has done very well in presenting a call to action for the Body of Christ at large, and to each member of that Body, a personal responsibility to ensure the carnal mind is subjected to the spirit man; so that the undiluted rivers of living water can pour from our spirits, through our souls, and out through our physical five senses to reach a hurting world that is desperate for a true, untainted touch from the Lord.

God has chosen in His infinite wisdom to work through His people to manifest His Son, the Lord Jesus Christ, to the world. This is an awesome responsibility that requires the utmost diligence on our part to harbor zealously that charge with reverential fear and a godly lifestyle. Since the kingdom of heaven resides in each of our spirits when we are born again, it is our privilege and duty to permit that kingdom to manifest throughout the earth in its most unsullied form. When Jesus prayed to His Father that "Your kingdom come, Your will be done, on earth and it is already done in heaven," I believe the primary fashion that Jesus expected this to happen was through the kingdom that resides in *us*, and thus His Father's will flowing out through us into the earth. We carry that spiritual kingdom with us wherever we go, with the eager expectation of seeing Christ's physical kingdom established in the near future.

This makes us co-laborers with Christ as well as co-heirs. This is both exhilarating and alarming. If one element of the team is weaker than the other, the whole team's production level suffers, right? We know that Jesus is perfect in every single way, so the fault lies with us if the kingdom is not manifested as He desires. That means you and I both have to make it a top priority that our expression of the kingdom in our daily lives is not thwarted or lessened, let's say, by the fruitless "vain imaginations" of an unregenerate mind, will and emotions. We are commanded to bring every thought into captivity to the obedience of Christ, tearing down any high thing that would dare to exalt itself against the knowledge of God. This command implies activity on our part, working with our Helper to tear strongholds down. It won't happen automatically. We have a work to do alongside the Holy Spirit, and this book helps us in that mandatory endeavor.

Rather than just highlighting a problem and then leaving the reader with questions and no answers, the following material lists systematically many of the "ways and means" of cooperating with the Holy Spirit's work in our lives to eradicate the leaven of situational ethics, secular Humanism, universalist thought, and the dangerous mixture of our carnal flesh—which must be crucified—with the pure, unadulterated power that is resident in each born again person's spirit.

The Bible makes it clear that we *can* be holy (set apart) before the Lord, only by yielding to His Word as it separates each facet of our existence—spirit, soul and body—into its components, identifying our thoughts and intents that must be subjected to that written Word. Only by submitting our day-to-day lives to the aggressive help of the Holy Spirit are we able to make the living Word most fruitful in our lives. It takes both the Word and the Spirit working together to achieve victory over the carnal mind. From that point, the Spirit has free rein to pour His life through us, out into the lives of others.

After reading this book, we are left without excuse to fulfill our Father's commandment: "Be holy, because I am holy." And by working with the Holy Spirit operating in our lives, we can achieve this lofty position in Christ Jesus. *The Carnal Mind* gives us a lot of spiritual keys toward this goal. When you read this book, I urge you not to approach it with an "I've got this all down" mindset—because *none* of us do. There are areas of our minds, wills and emotions that each of us must learn to surrender to the Spirit. Rather, be mindful, watchful, prayerful as you read it, asking the Holy Spirit to do His enlightening work in those areas of your life that must be yielded to Him. Don't be hypercritical of yourself—it is all a work of grace anyway. But also, don't forget that you play a vital role in overcoming the carnal mind! This book will help you fulfill that role.

—Andrew Maloney, author of the *Blue Time* series
Dove on the Rise International

PART 1

DEFINING THE PROBLEM

1

THE PROBLEM OF A CARNAL MIND

If we have been saved by grace, Ephesians 2:4-7 tells us that we are seated in heavenly places in Christ Jesus. The Bible also says that Christ has spoiled principalities and powers, triumphing over them. (Colossians 2:15) Other scripture makes it clear that through Christ, believers have been freed from the dominion of the evil one. And yet, at one point or another, all of us as Christians have felt like the victim—that we are beneath, and not above, the tail and not the head. Why is this? Why does it feel that sometimes our "faith" is just not working?

I believe one of the main reasons is that, as believers, it is easy for us to become "issues" oriented during our lifetime on earth. We hear and observe all the corruption and perversion of the culture of our time, and it becomes draining—we get bogged down with the cares of this world. Even with good intentions, a child of God may become so focused on trying to right the moral wrongs—to save a hopeless world and see justice prevail—that he or she has little time for anything else. So we become weary in well doing.

That's not to say we shouldn't care, that we shouldn't be active in confronting moral degradation as the Spirit directs. But what if the issues of this age serve as a Trojan horse of sorts for our adversary, distractions that keep us looking the other way? What if, while trying to stave off and even rescue some from the god of this world, the enemy has, through veils and smokescreens, invaded the very "temple of the Holy Ghost," the inner man of the believer?

The only actual power the adversary has over a born again believer is deception. From Genesis to the Book of Revelation, satan is described as an adversary with crafty strategies. Genesis 2 describes the serpent (satan) as the most cunning and subtle creature on earth. Revelation 12:9 calls satan the "deceiver of the whole world."

This doesn't change the fact, that yes, through the walk of faith, we are **more than** conquerors (Romans 8:37) and therefore, "more than" equipped for anything that comes our way. So, again, why do we sometimes feel that we are fighting a losing battle?

"...Because the mind of the flesh (with its carnal thoughts and purposes) is HOSTILE to GOD (enmity), for it (the mind of the flesh) does not SUBMIT itself (subject itself) to God's Law; indeed, it cannot." (Romans 8:7 AMP) (Emphasis added)

I'd like to challenge you that before you decide this isn't a book for you, as a dedicated believer, please think again. Obviously the topic of this book is the "carnal mind." By and far, I would prefer to teach and preach about all that God has accomplished and completed on our behalf through Christ Jesus and our position in Him. But it is part of the ministry of Holy Spirit to reveal **truth** to us, since He is the Spirit of Truth. (John 16:13) And the fact is, all of us *do* experience being deceived (mostly about ourselves!) at some point in our lives. It has been said that if you *think* you cannot be deceived, you are *already* deceived. Deception is a fruit of the pride of life: "the pride of your heart has deceived you...." (Obadiah 1:3 KJV)

Presumption, an aspect of pride, is one of the subtle contradictions of **faith**.

It is a self-righteous attitude ("I am right; this is not subject to discussion!") that blinds one to the Truth. It can be very persuasive, very charismatic, very forceful, even with the use of scripture; but it isn't teachable, correctable, by Holy Spirit. It is actually an exercise of one's mind, not of one's born again spirit.

So let's humble ourselves in the sight of the Lord (James 4:10) that the eyes of our heart may be enlightened. (Ephesians 1:18)

To begin to *consider the effect of the carnal mind upon a believer,* we need to clarify and define some words and phrases that we may not have given much attention to—or may *presume* are not talking about us!

These are general, but working, definitions taken from the Amplified Bible:

- *Flesh*—the entire nature of man (human nature) *without* (input) of the Holy Spirit (flesh being nature—not just the tissue and muscles on our bones)
- *Mind of flesh*—sense and reason *without* (input) of the Holy Spirit (called the "carnal mind" in KJV—the same definition and term we use in this book)
- *Carnal*—to be governed by senses and reason *without* (input) of the Holy Spirit
- *Lusts*—(our developed definition)—strong desire, though not necessarily wrong desire—desires under the power of our senses, not submitted to the Lord
- *Lusts of the flesh*—same as above—not necessarily immoral in nature, as many people interpret "flesh" to mean
- *Carnal nature*—referring to the old nature that by faith is dead through identifying with Christ in His death, yet used in reference to believers (see 1 Corinthians 3:1)

We find that when we mention the words *carnal, flesh* and *lusts,* many believers **presume** these are references to sexual or immoral behavior and somewhat dismiss any other understanding. If we don't consider what the Bible actually says in regard to these words, very little will be gained by reading this book.

The previously mentioned scripture refers to the believers at Corinth as "carnal." (KJV) That is "men of the flesh in whom the **carnal nature** predominates." (AMP) This is in spite of the fact that Paul is recorded as saying to the same people they were not lacking, did not fall behind, in any spiritual giftings. It is a somewhat common assumption that operating in spiritual gifts is the mark of spirituality, of some measure of spiritual maturity. But Paul's first statement in Chapter 3 makes it clear—this is not so!

"And I, brethren, could not speak to you as to spiritual people but as to carnal, as to babes in Christ." (1 Corinthians 3:1 NKJ) The Amplified adds "men of the flesh, in whom the carnal nature predominates." To paraphrase, then: "You operate in spiritual gifts... but you are carnal." Sounds like an oxymoron.

Suffice to say, yes, Spirit-filled, tongue-talking, faith-speaking, Word-reading, church-attending, praying and tithing believers can be **carnal**! The carnal nature can begin to flourish again, and with it comes the carnal mind.

One of the objections to this teaching is that, in Christ, we have a new nature. And this is true. Romans 6 states the doctrine of the new birth fairly completely. But it also contains Verse 16: "Do you not know that if you continually surrender yourselves to anyone: to do his will, you are the slaves of him whom you obey, whether that be to sin, which leads to death, or to obedience which leads to righteousness (right doing and right standing with God)?" (AMP) It is clear from the context that Paul is referring to surrendering to the old, carnal nature or the new nature.

Certainly your **new** nature isn't continually involved in obeying the old sin nature, but all of us *are* dealing with the old nature at some place, some time on earth, post salvation. So it must be the old nature trying to revive. If we want to live in freedom as sons of God, we must pursue the revelation in the Word about developing and living from the new nature. Without doing so, we will, by default, continue to live from the old nature.

"But I say, walk and live [habitually] in the [Holy] Spirit [responsive to and controlled and guided by the Spirit]; then you will certainly not gratify the cravings and desires of the flesh (of human nature without God).For the desires of the flesh are opposed to the [Holy] Spirit, and the [desires of the] Spirit are opposed to the flesh (godless human nature); for these are antagonistic to each other [continually withstanding and in conflict with each other], so that you are not free but are prevented from doing what you desire to do." (Galatians 5:16-17 AMP)

The KJV says, "For the flesh lusteth against the Spirit, and the Spirit against the flesh: and these are contrary the one to the other..."

"Whereby are given unto us exceeding great and precious promises: that **by these** (promises) ye might be **partakers** of the divine nature, having escaped the corruption that is in the world through lust." (2 Peter 1:4 KJV; author emphasis added) This scripture seems to indicate that the difference in a *doctrine of the new* nature—and the *experiencing of the new nature*—has much to do with the Word and faith.

Galatians 4:31 makes it clear that in the new birth, we have been **freed** from the old nature that sin and death held sway over. Galatians 5:1 then admonishes us to **stand fast**, firm in our freedom and liberty from the spiritual law of sin and death. *Stand fast* in our new life and walk in the *Spirit* (new nature.) So why the admonition, if there is no possibility of reverting back to the old nature?

The terminology of "stand" and "walk" indicates a *way of life* that is drawn forth from the superior, unseen realm of the *Spirit*. It speaks of a "living way"—not a one-time experience. Our freewill must be exercised to partake of and participate in this superior realm of the kingdom of God. As born again sons of God, we are free to choose, like Adam. But choose we must, if we want to live in our completed salvation while still on earth. Not to choose is to default to the lower, natural earthbound life...and the carnal mind.

"There is therefore now no condemnation to those who are in Christ Jesus, who do not walk according to the flesh, but according to the Spirit. For the law of the Spirit of life in Christ Jesus has made me free from the law of sin and death." (Romans 8:1-2 NKJ)

"Why should not the dispensation of the Spirit [this spiritual ministry whose task it is to cause men to obtain and be governed by the Holy Spirit] be attended with much greater and more splendid glory?" (2 Corinthians 3:8 AMP)

This scripture states that it is the **task** (assignment) of the Holy Spirit to cause men to obtain and be **governed by the Holy Spirit**.

This is in contrast to the old nature—flesh, senses, reason, logic—that governs the natural man, the carnal mind.

"So that the righteous and just requirement of the Law might be fully met in us who live and move not in the ways of the flesh but in the ways of the Spirit [our lives governed not by the standards and according to the dictates of the flesh, but controlled by the Holy Spirit]." (Romans 8:4 AMP)

Note how "moving in the ways of the Spirit" is in contrast to "moving in the ways of the flesh"—also note the use of the word **governed** once again. This also seems to be an accepted understanding of Romans 8:14: "For all who are led by the Spirit of God are sons of God." (AMP) The KJV says "For as many as are led by the Spirit of God, they are the sons of God." The word *governed* in place of the term "led by" brings clarification.

So even though anyone who has put their faith in Jesus' completed work for their justification and redemption are truly "sons of God," this scripture compared with others seems to be referring to the "mature" sons of God—those who are governed by the Spirit, who live and move in the ways of the Spirit (new nature.)

This is a theme we will develop further on in the book, but briefly stated from the 1 Corinthians 3:1-3 portion, those who are "governed" by the carnal mind are referred to by Paul as "babes." He calls them "of the flesh, mere unchanged men." (AMP) He wasn't only referring to the moral issues, but the things that many believers accept as normal life: strife, divisions, envying, and so on, as well as fear and anxiety. Galatians 5:19-21 gives a pretty comprehensive list also.

He is not speaking of what we would consider a "true babe" in Christ—one who is still in the first stages of growth according to chronological spiritual age, but of one who should *by now* be somewhat matured and able to walk after the Spirit.

This would seem to be especially true of the Corinthians, given they were partakers and participants of the workings of the Holy Spirit through the spiritual gifts. But they seemed to be disinterested in being *governed* by the Spirit in terms of daily life.

And perhaps to clarify the term "governed," we are not speaking of an inner *dominance* of the Holy Spirit, but of an inner *yielding* to Him in the heart, as hence, one would be *governed* by Him. The Holy Spirit, as God in us, waits for us to give Him the invitation and permission to act in this capacity in our lives. **If we walk after the Spirit, we will not fulfill the lusts (desires) of the flesh. (Again, Galatians 5:16.)**

The spiritual law of sin and death spoken of in Romans 8:2 is like gravity. It is always in effect. You cannot really break or alter the law of gravity. In fact, if one should attempt to break the law of gravity, he or she would only end up *proving* the law of gravity...what goes up *will* come down. Yet man has discovered that by superseding gravity, going to a higher natural law, they can indeed "go up" and "stay up"—being under the effect of the higher law of "lift and thrust." Man can fly in aircraft by activating and operating in the higher law of aerodynamics.

If we view the spiritual law stated in Romans 8:2 as gravity, and lift and thrust, we will have a greater understanding of the new life in Christ Jesus. Yes, all analogies to earth do break down; but suffice to say that "lift and thrust" is by *choice* and must be activated and maintained—and gravity is the default that will prevail, unless superseded.

2
ONLY TWO WAYS

One observation in studying this subject is that from God's point of view, there are only two ways, two minds, two masters, two walks, two main spiritual laws, two sources of strength, two natures... and we could go on. You will find this truth throughout God's Word. It is deception to think that because you have a "choice," a third option is created. The choice is between domination by the carnal mind, or yielding to the mind of the Spirit revealed in the Word of God.

"NO ONE can SERVE TWO MASTERS; for either he will hate the one and love the other; or he will stand by and be devoted to the one and despise and be against the other." (Matthew 6:24 AMP) The Word then references God and mammon. "Mammon" doesn't speak only of money and possessions; it speaks of whatever is trusted in, relied upon. I think the word **rely** actually creates a better understanding regarding Mammon.

Through many years of ministry and experience, my husband and I have found that it appears you can *seemingly not really commit* to a life lived by faith, from the new nature, for many years. But whatever you have been relying on will *ultimately exercise control* over you... just as the Word says... *no one* can serve two masters.

From the Old Testament, it is pretty well known how God feels about "mixture." In a believer's walk, mixture is a myth—it is the "myth of neutrality." It is the myth that there is a *third* way called "my way." The thought is somewhat like a food buffet: I get to choose, so I will *choose* some of the Word and Spirit—and I will choose some of the things of the (not-so-bad) flesh.

For a believer, the myth of mixture and neutrality could be called attrition. Slowly, almost unperceivably, taking a toll, but not very noticeably at any one point. Perhaps the words "subtle, cunning" would apply here. We don't *think* this is a problem. But when the Word says, "No man can serve two masters"—meaning it's *not* possible—then that is the **truth**. You *cannot* in reality. Maybe in virtual reality. But in real life, one will eventually master you.

We had a little boy in our Christian school who always liked to raise his hand and say what was on his mind. One day he raised his hand and said, "I don't want to listen to God or the devil; I just want them *both* to leave me alone." The myth of mixture and neutrality. Notice it came from a child in the first grade. Perhaps this line of thought relates to what Paul was calling "babes."

I believe what will clarify the division, or separation, of the "carnal mind" and the "mind of the Spirit" can be found in Jeremiah 17:5-8 (NKJ):

"Thus says the Lord: 'Cursed is the man who trusts in man and makes flesh his strength, whose heart departs from the Lord. For he shall be like a shrub in the desert, and shall not see when good comes, but shall inhabit the parched places in the wilderness, in a salt land which is not inhabited. Blessed is the man who trusts in the Lord, and whose hope is the Lord. For he shall be like a tree planted by the waters, which spreads out its roots by the river, and will not fear when heat comes; but its leaf will be green, and will not be anxious in the year of drought, nor will cease from yielding fruit."

The scripture flat-out states that those who *"rely on"* (AMP) the arm of flesh (the strength of man) will live under a curse. It states that those who *"rely on"* the Lord will live under the blessings of God. By the way, this is another example of the "twos."

Yes, I know this is Old Testament, and I know and believe that Christ has purchased my freedom, redeemed me from the curse. Yes, I know and believe Numbers 23:23 (which, by the way, is also *Old Testament.*) No one can reverse the blessings spoken by God by means of a spoken curse.

If we really consider life on earth, we must acknowledge that *reliance* isn't something you do just once in your lifetime, but it is a continuing action of the heart and will.

As Galatians 3 states, Christ has redeemed us from the curse by becoming a curse on our behalf. Galatians 4 and 5 continue to teach and exhort that we must *stand and walk* in the freedom to remain free. So let's look at this truth demonstrated in the Old Testament—especially if we are going to consider Numbers 23.

3

TRUST AND BELIEVE

The words "trust in and believe" in both the Old and New Testaments often carry the meaning of "rely on." In the Amplified version you see these words used as synonyms. It seems to me that the word "rely" is much more concrete for our time than the words "trust and believe." In cases where the word "rely" is actually used, it carries the meaning of "lean on."

Second Chronicles 15 and 16 are vivid examples of this principle. In this scenario, King Asa received a directional word from the prophet and acted upon it. He led his kingdom into seeking the Lord with all their hearts. The Lord heard and delivered them from their enemies, and they had twenty years of peace. Sometimes the "good life" provided by the Lord leads to passivity and presumption.

After twenty years, another enemy arose. But this time, rather than *seek* the Lord, King Asa *sought human strength*, human alliances; and his enemy escaped him.

Verses 7 and 8 of Chapter 16 state this: "...*Because you relied* on the king of Syria—and not on the Lord, the army of the king of Syria has escaped you. Were not the Ethiopians and Libyans a huge host with very many chariots and horsemen? Yet *because you relied* on the Lord, He gave them into your hand." (AMP)

Next let us consider verse 9, a very well-known scripture, "For the eyes of the Lord run to and fro throughout the whole earth to show

Himself strong in behalf of those whose hearts are blameless toward Him." (2 Chronicles 16:9 AMP)

Now, pause a moment here. Did God just change subjects on us, or is He still talking about "relying" on Him? Was this just abstractly thrown in or what?

Keep reading... "You have done *foolishly* in this [reference previous scriptures] therefore, from now on you shall have wars."

The seer Hanani was pointing out to Asa (and us) what causes God to come on the scene in full strength: it is FULLY RELYING (leaning on) on Him. That is also referenced as a "heart that is blameless toward Him." If you aren't sure about that, keep reading.

Verse 10: "Then [because of what Hanani was telling him] Asa was angry with the seer..." So Asa didn't want to hear it, and he didn't want to repent. See, something had happened to Asa's *heart* during the twenty years of peace. Jeremiah 17:5 says, in reference to those who *rely* on the strength of man, their *heart and mind* (AMP) *have departed from the Lord.* This "attrition" can be very subtle.

Continuing on, "Then Asa was angry with the seer and put him in prison for he was enraged [sounds like the carnal mind!] with him because of this. Asa oppressed some of the people at the same time."

Very sad, this man who had led his kingdom to seek the Lord with all their heart—now rejecting the word of the prophet and oppressing his people. Ultimately (see Verse 12) Asa became diseased in his feet until his disease became very severe; yet in his disease he did not seek the Lord, but *relied* on the physicians. (And just a note here—we're not saying people shouldn't see doctors. However, there is a huge divide between consulting a physician and *relying* on a physician.)

Who and what we are relying on isn't difficult to ascertain for one who is honestly wanting to know. We are talking about receiving correction and instruction from the Word, being teachable, which is *not* an attribute of the carnal mind. Remember Romans 8:7: "The carnal mind is an enemy of God; it does not *submit* to God."

And there's a little more we can learn from Asa in Chapter 15. The original message of the prophet to King Asa: "The Lord is with you while you are with Him." (Verse 2) Hmmm. "*If you seek Him* (as your soul's first necessity, that is, in reliance), He will be found by you. But if you (become indifferent) and forsake Him, He will forsake you." (AMP, paraphrase)

To glean from the entire record of events in Asa's life, we must connect the original word given to him with what Hanani the seer said to him twenty years later. Again, we see the "twos." There weren't three options given, only two.

The message seems to be, If you are *seeking* Me (because you rely on Me), then, you are *with* Me. If you *stop* seeking Me (stop relying on Me), then, you have *forsaken* Me... therefore, I have forsaken you. This is the principle for the covenant believer—the Lord is always the LORD. He never forsakes us—He is the Absolute; He is the eternal, unchangeable One. But He responds to us, to our faith, which I believe is most clearly stated in the words "rely on, lean on." This takes the concept out of the often-muddied mental realm into the "acting upon" realm of life. Faith, reliance upon, *acts* upon the Word. Mental assent *talks* the Word.

"But be ye doers of the Word and not hearers only, deceiving your own selves." (James 1:22 KJV)

In Micah 3:11-12 (KJV), the actions of the judges, priests, and prophets were clearly for personal gain and of the "carnal mind"—leaning on the arm of flesh. "The heads thereof judge for reward, and the priests thereof teach for hire, and the prophets thereof divine for money...." Their deceived state of mind is revealed in the following: "...Yet will they lean upon the Lord and say, Is not the Lord among us? None evil can come upon us. Therefore, shall Zion for your sake (because of you) be plowed as a field, and Jerusalem shall become heaps, and the mountain of the house as the high places of the forest."

Sounds like the mixture; the deception of thinking you can rely on the arm of flesh, believing that your words of confidence will activate the arm of the Lord on your behalf. If the Word of God is *absolute truth*—it won't happen that way.

It is a presumptuous mistake to view our completed salvation in the Kingdom of God as *merely* a fact on earth. Our salvation isn't *fact*—as we would view something from the earth realm. Rather, our completed salvation is *faith*. It is born of faith, and it is lived and sustained by faith. This may have been lost in the overemphasis of "faith for" the things we need for "earthlife." We have two options in life when it comes to reliance—the old nature or the new nature. But we cannot expect people to "stop relying on the old nature" unless we accompany that with revelation about relying on the new nature.

4

GROWING IN CHRIST

Through the knowledge of Christ and His exceedingly great and precious promises... we *become partakers of His Divine Nature*. (2 Peter 1:3-4 AMP)

"...But *grow in the grace and knowledge of our Lord and Savior Jesus Christ*..." (2 Peter 3:18 NKJV)

I believe we can take from these two passages in 2 Peter that there is a "growing" into actually being governed by the *nature of Christ*. It is the difference from the legal sense and the vital, or experiential, sense. We are speaking of that which develops in the heart/soul realm. We are born again spiritually, *in our spirit*, and nothing affects that short of an all-out, total renouncing of Jesus. But we are spirit, soul and body. (1 Thessalonians 5:23) The soul (heart, mind, will, emotions) is the "land" to be "possessed" by the new nature of the believer.

The simple reality is that our soul (heart) has full access to the life of God through the Person of Holy Spirit. And through the living Word of God, we have access to "all things that pertain to life and godliness." (2 Peter 1:3) Our soul (heart) is where the nature of a person will either be influenced by sense and reason without the Spirit (that is, the carnal mind)—*or* it will be influenced by the entire reality of the realm of the Kingdom of God, to which we have ACCESS.

"Therefore, having been justified by faith, we have peace with God through our Lord Jesus Christ, through whom also we have *access by faith* into this grace...." (Romans 5:1-2 NKJV)

Jesus said, "If you abide in Me and My words abide in you..." Notice there is an *if*—that can only be fulfilled by the choices and obedience of those who have been influenced, fully persuaded, and won over to the superiority of the realm of the Spirit. Glory to glory—faith to faith—strength to strength—grace upon grace. This speaks of a "transformational process" (Roman 12:2) by the renewing of the mind, for the purpose of not being "conformed" to this world system.

In Romans 8:5-8, Paul identifies and addresses the "two" minds. They are spoken of as "the mind of the flesh or carnal mind" and the "mind of the spirit or spiritually minded." Let's clarify that when we say "spiritually minded," we aren't talking about being "religiously minded." We aren't talking about confession cops, self-righteous rules, external extremes, etc.

"The proof that our religion is very much that of the religious flesh is that sinful flesh will be found to flourish along with it. Religious flesh and sinful flesh are one! No wonder that with a great deal of religion, temper and selfishness and worldliness are so often found side by side. The religion of the flesh cannot conquer sin." (Andrew Murray, *The Two Covenants*)

I call it the pendulum of "good flesh" and "bad flesh"—but nevertheless, it *is* flesh, the carnal nature, the mind of sense, reason and logic without Holy Spirit.

"When pride cometh, then shame cometh." (Proverbs 11:2 KJV) The religiously observant flesh causes self-righteousness to swell, but the same flesh will then flail you for *not succeeding* in your performance, not being PERFECT. Then the self-rejection and self-condemnation set in to punish you till you feel you have sufficiently paid penance and are "better," at which time the pendulum begins to swing back again, toward pride and presumption.

We have pastored for a long time... seen many pendulum swings, both personally and in our congregations. It is a truly miserable way to live, while all the time loving the Lord and desiring to serve Him, to be used of Him for the Kingdom of God. It is the taskmaster spirit of religious flesh, a strong indicator that the carnal mind is ruling in place of the mind of the Spirit.

Remember the tree that Adam and Eve were not to partake of was the Tree of Knowledge of Good and Evil. Knowledge of "good" cannot deliver you from the power of the carnal nature. It can assist in temporarily modifying your behavior, but the lusts of the flesh will return with a vengeance, somewhat like a boomerang.

Much emphasis is placed upon behavior modification in the church, without actually calling it such. It is emphasis placed upon the outward man, performance, compliance, rules—rather than the inward man, the hidden man of the heart. But scripture (Mark 7:20-23) tells us that all that corrupts and defiles a man comes from the inner man.

I would call this a "failed policy" of religion; it has accomplished nothing, nor will it accomplish anything in actually addressing the carnal mind/carnal nature. Good flesh—against bad flesh... is powerless. In fact, it strengthens the fleshly, carnal nature as it appeals to the pride and desire of that nature for control. But it is more "religious" in behavior than "sinful" in behavior. What is born of the flesh is flesh, what is born of the spirit is spirit.

So yes, we are talking about the "heart." It isn't difficult to understand that when you study words, you will find that "heart" is sometimes translated from words meaning spirit or sometimes from words meaning soul. From my studies, I believe when you compare scripture with scripture, you will find the heart to be part of the soul realm, separate from the spirit. Ezekiel 37:26, speaking of the New Covenant, did say, "A new heart I will give you *and* a new spirit."

So how does that compare with other scriptures? One scripture that I feel is foundational regarding the heart is Proverbs 4:23 (KJV): "Keep your heart with all diligence, for out of *it* spring the *issues of life.*" The Amplified says "above all that you guard," and uses "springs of life" for "issues of life." But ISSUES speak pretty clearly to our time. The point is, the *heart* is identified as the center of the life of man. Consider these scriptures:

"...For as he *thinks in his heart*, so is he." (Proverbs 23:7 NKJV) Hmmm, indicating our "thinking" is coming from our heart, not our mind.

"The heart is deceitful above all things, and desperately wicked; who can know it?" (Jeremiah 17:9 KJV) Could it be that once we have received our "new heart" in Christ, we haven't learned, haven't been taught, that we must GUARD it diligently? That it can once again become corrupted and therefore, of course, your mind will become corrupted. We like to say, "Well, God knows my heart..." Indeed, He does. But **we don't**.

"Where your treasure is, *there* will your heart be also." (Matthew 6:21 KJV) Going on, it talks about the single eye and not serving two masters. I believe the word "treasure" is closely linked to the word "mammon" in Verse 24.

"For out of the fullness (the overflow, the superabundance) of the heart, the mouth speaks." (Matthew 12:34 AMP) Yes, we can certainly modify our speech when and where we decide to do so. But ultimately, out of the "superabundance of the storehouse of the heart," the mouth will overflow. It isn't about what comes out of your mouth when you are around the pastor that matters; it is what "overflows" from the heart through your mouth when you just can't contain it anymore. *That* is at issue.

"But whatever comes out of the mouth comes from the heart, and this is what makes a man unclean and defiles him." (Matthew 15:18 AMP)

I think the above could be summed up somewhat by saying that we can only **know** our own hearts by checking the fruit.

- What we treasure the MOST—will reveal our heart
- What we think on the MOST—will reveal our heart
- What we speak about the MOST—will reveal our heart
- What we rely on the MOST—will reveal our heart

So if we return to the concept of "twos," there are two sources from which our heart is influenced: 1) sense and reason without the Spirit (this is called carnal); or 2) the influence of the unseen, superior realm of the Spirit, the Kingdom of God, by the Living Word of God and Holy Spirit.

We have *access* into this spirit realm, this **grace** by faith—the Spirit of God, the Living Word of God. He has given to us, made accessible to us, all things that pertain to life and godliness through the knowledge of Christ and His exceedingly great and precious promises.

We must truly **choose life**. Jesus said, "The words that I speak unto you, they are *spirit and they are life*." (John 6:63 KJV)

I would like to offer that the new nature, the new creation, that Paul speaks of in Ephesians is the life-giving Spirit of God that comes when you are born again. It is "incorruptible." "Born again, not of corruptible seed, but of incorruptible, by the word of God, which liveth and abideth forever." (1 Pet 1:23 KJV)

It is the heart of man that is subject to corruption—and must be joined to the Lord—to be one spirit, one nature, during earthlife, if it is to be governed by the Spirit.

"For with the *heart*, man believeth ("relies on Christ," AMP) unto **righteousness**, and with the mouth confession is made unto salvation." (Romans 10:10)

PART 2

EXAMINING THE FRUIT

5

ISHMAEL VERSUS ISAAC

opefully, as we have looked over scripture regarding the "mind of the flesh (carnal)" and the "mind of the spirit," we have come to realize it is very relevant, and the scriptures are talking to us!

Many have stated that "the mind is the battlefield." The "mind of the flesh" actually starts from the outside with the senses, reason and logic, and influences our heart from that realm. And it is indeed, a battlefield.

But if we don't realize that the "mind of the **Spirit**" *doesn't* start with the organ of the brain, we will continue to struggle in some religious futility and eventually feel more like a victim than a victor during our life on earth. I have heard many people say, "Well, I get it (truth) in my mind, but it just hasn't dropped into my heart." I don't believe that is based on scriptural principle—rather it is a seemingly acceptable excuse offered by the carnal mind itself.

The natural mind does not, cannot, receive the things of the Spirit. (1 Corinthians 2:14) Yes, the natural mind can somewhat comprehend the *words* of the Bible when read in a version written in their native language, and certainly, study aids with definitions from the Greek and Hebrew are helpful.

But the above scripture says that to the natural man, things of the Spirit of God (His Word is Spirit) are *foolishness* and therefore *unwelcome to natural man*. And it goes on to explain why... Because the mind of the natural man (based on sense, reason, logic) cannot know, is incapable of knowing and discerning, the things of the Spirit. Amplified says the things of the Spirit are folly, meaningless nonsense, to the natural mind—or as Romans 8 says, the mindset of the flesh.

This is a predicament for those who believe and want to read the Bible—but actually lean on the sense, logic, intellect of the natural mind to interpret what they read.

The Word of God is written from a totally different "mindset," if you please, than natural man. Jesus did say, "The Words that I speak are spirit..." (John 6:63)

I think this gives clarification to Romans 8:7, which states that the mind of the flesh does not, will not, *cannot* be subject to or submit to God for it is at enmity with Him; its thoughts and purposes are hostile to God. This actually restates what Roman 6 points out—a death must take place to the old nature and its thinking, not a rehabilitation.

This revelation could be quite disconcerting if we don't study on because it messes with the armor of spirituality in which we have placed our trust. We may think, if the carnal mind doesn't submit to God, then *what am I to do?!*

We may even discover at some point that we were actually exercising "mind over matter," which starts with the head, rather than acting on faith in God's Word, which starts with the heart.

If we study the Word of God but don't know how the natural, carnal mind works to offer us a "reasonable" understanding of the scripture, we won't realize we have become our own worst enemy. The Word calls it "deceiving our own selves by reasoning contrary to the word" in James 1:22. (AMP) It is set in the context of **doing**... acting upon, relying upon, the Word that we hear.

But we know that our "doing" must be in **faith**. Faith is of the Spirit—and the carnal mind cannot *receive or discern* the things of the Spirit.

Neither does it mean that I am a puppet with Holy Spirit pulling the strings. Our walk in the Spirit is truly a cooperative effort with the Lord as stated in 2 Corinthians 6:1 (KJV) "We, then, as workers together with him (God), beseech you also that ye receive not the grace of God in vain."

This follows the scripture that outlines the complete vicarious exchange made through Christ on our behalf. He became (legally) sin; and we who believe became (legally) righteous, the grace to which we have full access for our full life on earth—that is, to come into a fullness of the expression of Christ Himself and His Kingdom on earth.

So with **all the resources of God *for us,* how could anything possibly stand against us?!**

I think we will find that only one person can ultimately keep us in a position of minimizing, neutralizing the power of God that lies mostly dormant and untapped within us—and that person is the one we look at in the mirror.

"My people are destroyed for lack of knowledge." (Hosea 4:6 NKJV) This was spoken to Israel, the priesthood nation. Going on it states that they, Israel, had rejected knowledge ... and He would reject them.

Notice again, as in speaking to Asa (2 Chronicles 15), God responded to *their* response to His grace. The character and nature of God and His great mercy never changes, but these portions of the scripture reemphasize that God has given, provided, *all* things that pertain to life and godliness. He never alters His Word; He never changes His thoughts and plans for a people called out. But He never transgresses their right and responsibility to *choose* whom they will serve.

Two in the house. Here it is again, the principle of "twos"!

"For it is written that Abraham had two sons, one by the bondmaid and one by the free woman. Whereas the child of the slave woman was born according to the flesh, the son of the free woman was born in fulfillment of the promise. Now this is an allegory; these two women represent two covenants." (Galatians 4:22-24 AMP)

"But we, brethren, are children like Isaac, born in virtue of promise. Just as at that time the child born according to the flesh despised and persecuted him born according to the promise, the Spirit, so it is now also. But what does the Scripture say? Cast out and send away the slave woman and her son, for never shall the son of the slave woman be heir and share the inheritance with the son of the free woman. So brethren, we who are born again are not children of a slave woman, the natural, but of the free, the supernatural." (Galatians 4:28-31 AMP)

"In this freedom Christ has made us free; stand fast then, and do not be hampered and held ensnared and submit once again to a yoke of slavery, which you have once put off." (Galatians 5:1 AMP)

To put this in context, Paul is not just referring to the Law—he is referring to the life that is called "slavery"—being of only natural birth. Look at Verse 31 again, and you will see it. Verse 29 states that "even as it was at that time, so it is now," referring to the reality of "that which is born of the flesh persecutes that which is born of the spirit."

This accounts for the many needless struggles that we experience in our walk as a believer, thinking it is normal.

But it is only "*normal wilderness*" mentality, the bondage and slavery we put upon ourselves through unbelief. The children of Israel wouldn't *enter in* to what was prepared for them. We don't *enter in* to what is prepared for us. More on this later.

Often when we read portions that speak of the Law that Israel was under, we think, I am not under the Law so this doesn't pertain to menu. We absolutely are not under the Old Covenant Law; furthermore, we never have been. Christ fulfilled the Law and made an end to it as a means for righteousness. However, Galatians 4 is referring to that which is "born of the flesh" and that which is "born of the spirit." For a time, both lived in the house with Abraham, but the time came when one had to be sent away, and it is good to make note and learn.

It's an allegory for both natures living in a believer. Your body "houses" you, the spirit man. That which is born of the flesh, as in Ishmael (we could call this the good, religious flesh) will always persecute that which is born of the spirit. The time came when the house could no longer accommodate both natures. One had to exert authority over the other; one had to be **cast out**! (Not meaning as in "casting out" demons, but the new nature governing and evicting the old nature.)

The "free" is the one born of the incorruptible seed of the Word of God, which lives and abides forever. (1 Peter 1:23) The "free one" that is born again of the Spirit has power and authority over that which is the slave, born only of the flesh. The time comes when the "free" must no longer give the spirit of slavery a place to occupy. **Evict it!**

"...we are debtors but not to the flesh..." (Romans 8:12 AMP)

"...make no provision for the flesh..." (Romans 13:14 AMP)

"...put no confidence in the flesh..." (Philippians 3:3 AMP)

Often believers become focused on fighting "evil"—a perception that "evil" is the source of all the problems on earth. And, typically, that evil is defined along the lines of morality. But we forget that the forbidden tree was the tree of knowledge of *good and evil*. Yes, the carnal nature can be "good" in behavior, "good" in speaking, "good" in some moral ways. And we have a tendency to think that anything that is "good"—can't be "evil." Just keep in mind the pendulum—good flesh/bad flesh...it's all flesh. It is still part of the tree that was forbidden.

"For being ignorant of the righteousness that God ascribes and seeking to establish a righteousness of their own, they did not obey or submit themselves to God's righteousness." (Romans 10:3 AMP) The "good" part of the tree is exposed in this scripture. Self-righteousness is the definition of "seeking to establish a righteousness of their own." It encompasses all the self-efforts and energy expended to deal with the nagging feelings of insignificance and self-worth, somehow thinking our old nature conscience can be purged by our performing.

6

Recognizing the "Other" Gospel

*F*or I am zealous for you with a godly eagerness and a divine jealousy, for I have betrothed you to one Husband, to present you as a chaste virgin to Christ." (2 Corinthians 11:2 AMP)

"But I am fearful lest that even as the serpent beguiled (thoroughly deceived) Eve by his cunning (appeal by wise and tasty use of words and logic), so your minds may be corrupted and seduced from wholehearted, sincere and pure devotion (simplicity) to Christ." (2 Corinthians 11:3 AMP—author paraphrase added)

What did the serpent use to beguile Eve? The tree of knowledge of good and evil; a tree that was good for food, pleasant to the eyes, and to be desired to make one wise. Could we say appealing to the senses—and the power of the mind to reason?

We must understand this: the "good" of the tree of knowledge of good and evil—is only *relevant* good. It is "good" based on what it does for the individual who is making the judgment of good and evil. If it accommodates the individual's interests and life plan, if it furthers his goals and lines his pockets, it is good! If it doesn't require too much of him, then that is good... The "good life here and now," according to the Secular Humanists.

We can no more compare the "Godly Good"—*good* in reference to our Holy God—with this "good," than you can compare the Tree of Life with the Tree of Knowledge of Good and Evil. The carnal mind doesn't have the capacity to know and appreciate anything as being "good"—apart from the personal benefits derived from that "good."

And today it has the same appeal. Paul was still addressing the church at Corinth—the same one that he said was "yet carnal." Perhaps the answer to the questions we have been proposing lies firmly in these few scriptures here from Paul.

"For you seem readily to endure it if a man comes and preaches another Jesus than the one we preached, or if you receive a different spirit...or a different gospel...you tolerate it well enough!" (2 Corinthians 11:4 AMP)

He said to the church at Corinth that they were willing to put up with, tolerate, a different Jesus... a different Spirit... a different Gospel.

This parallels Galatians 4—two in the house. Tolerating an influence and force that antagonizes, persecutes and compromises the absolute of the Kingdom of God in the Spirit—like adding alloy to precious metal.

The Gospel Paul presented had one central truth—simplicity (singleness) of devotion to Jesus Christ in principle and practice; all that He was, all that He accomplished on behalf of mankind, and all that He taught.

A couple of other scripture portions expound on what Paul was thinking.

"I am surprised and astonished that you are so quickly turning renegade and deserting Him who invited and called you by the grace of Christ and that you are transferring your allegiance to a different ("another," KJV), even opposition, gospel." (Galatians 1:6 AMP)

Most of us would think he was talking about the church of satan, the occult, those churches that don't believe in Jesus as God. And these would be the fruit of that "gospel." But there is something bigger here than what we have seen. Paul clarifies in Verse 7: "Not that there could be any other Gospel," and Verses 8 and 9 referencing this "different" gospel.

Then in Verses 10-11, Paul hits the nail on the head. "Now am I trying to win the *favor of men* or of God? Do I seek to *please men*? If I were still seeking popularity with *men*, I should not be a bondservant of Christ. For I want you to know, brethren, that the Gospel which was proclaimed and made known by me is not *man's gospel*, a *human* invention patterned after any *human* standard." (That is, it's not born of the carnal mind.) AMP

"But just as we have been approved by God to be entrusted with the glad tidings (Gospel), so we speak not to please men but to please God, Who tests our hearts. For as you well know, we never resorted either to words of flattery or to any cloak to conceal greedy motives or pretexts for gain, as God is our witness. Nor did we seek to extract praise and honor and glory from men, either from you or from anyone else...." (1 Thessalonians 2:4-5 AMP)

What is the "different" (another) gospel that Paul was talking about? Could it possibly have any influence in *my* life? I go to church regularly, I pray, I tithe, I quote the Word, I am born again, I speak in tongues... and I certainly believe in Jesus!

To state it very simply, the "different gospel" is a "gospel" that is **centered on man**. I think most believers *assume* that they are **centered**

on God, particularly if their life is very involved with the church, the Word, Holy Spirit, perhaps even miracles, signs and wonders.

When we use the word "centered," we are once again referring to the heart, as the center of man, the place from where everything in our lives flows.

As we have mentioned, this different gospel has been around at least since the Garden, as far as its effects on man. But the origin would be traced to the five "I wills" of Lucifer in Isaiah 14. "You have said in your **heart**... *I will*..." (Verse 13)

It is the age old conflict of who is the supreme being—who is GOD? We may not have considered it this way, but when Jesus "freed" you from the powers of darkness, you were for the first time, truly free... which carries the awesome responsibility of "who you will now serve."

We are not so deceived so as to think that the archenemy of God, satan, is by any means *not* still actively involved in a campaign to overthrow the supremacy of our sovereign God. However, we know scripturally that a believer must be somehow persuaded to think and act in ways contrary to the Truth if satan is to have an *opportunity* to exercise his influence in our lives.

Francis Shaeffer studied and wrote at length about Secular Humanism. In his book *The God Who is There* he states, "The Christian is to resist the spirit of the world. But when we say this, we must understand that the world-spirit does not always take the same form. So the Christian must resist the spirit of the world *in the form it takes in his own generation*. If he does not do this, he is not resisting the spirit of the world at all. This is especially so for our generation, as the forces at work against us are of such a total nature."

He went on to say that the Christian must understand what opposes him in his own moment of history, else he becomes a useless museum piece and not a living warrior for Jesus Christ.

I believe he is referring somewhat to the Trojan Horse effect—not recognizing the form the enemy takes as he seeks ways to infiltrate and affect the Body of Christ.

7

Secular Humanism

Without question, those who have studied into "secular humanism" realize that this is the *form* that the world spirit is taking in our generation. For those who may not be so acquainted with the workings of this "world spirit," I would like to offer some facts that may be enlightening.

But first, may I say our beloved mentor in the Lord, John G. Garlock, imparted much wisdom to us. Perhaps the quote that has been the most powerful guidance is this: "It is more important to know what you are *for*—than what you are *against*." That statement is so about new creation realities and the Kingdom of God!

I use this quote frequently because I feel that the Body of Christ has been deceived into fighting "against" the world and the evils thereof, rather than embodying and extending what we are "for"—the completed work of Christ and His Kingdom in the earth, which is the only true deliverance from these evils. Submitting to God, resisting (not fighting) the devil....as you have heard it said in competitive sports......the best defense—is a strong offense!"

The meaning of "resist" (James 4:7) is to "take a 180 degree, contrary position, to keep one's possession, to forcefully declare one's personal conviction."

As I have grown in the Word and Spirit, my personality has changed. As a teen, I was shy and quiet, very self-conscious, meaning very conscious of what everyone thought of me and what they thought

I should do. This was especially true in my church world. As I have matured in my walk with the Lord, I am more of an aggressive activist, living from the inner man, my relationship with the Lord, rather than the outer man, my relationship with people.

However, for a number of years, I thought I was to use that passion to fight against the effects of humanism in the world in whatever form those effects presented to me. I studied and became well acquainted with the evils of humanism; but regardless of how organized and well-concerted the efforts have been, little change has come to our world through many years of people fighting against this spirit by man's methods and resources. There were many court battles surrounding the issue of humanism in our schools, in our textbooks, in society. But ultimately, the battle is spiritual; and all the best efforts of well-meaning believers will not prevail in the hearts and minds of men. Rules, regulations and more emphasis on morality than on a heart relationship with the Lord will prove to be futile.

Eventually, I came to realize that I was missing the mark—fighting against the evil rather than using my passion to develop and demonstrate the only remedy against humanism, the Kingdom of God. Many believers have been drawn in to thinking that we can actually use "flesh against flesh" and win the war. But most will just sort of give up and say "oh well"—or the passionate ones will burn themselves out for a losing cause. "Though we walk in the flesh, we do not war according to the flesh, for the weapons of our warfare are not carnal ..." (1 Corinthians 10:3 NKJV)

I haven't changed subjects here—I just want to be abundantly clear. The reason I am going to present knowledge about secular humanism is to help **awaken** the sleeping giant. There is a REASON that the church is ineffective in the world today. There is a reason that the Body of Christ sometimes doesn't experience any more victory over the problems of life than those who are not believers.

Jesus said, "You are the light of the world." (Matthew 5:14 NKJV) He also said, "If therefore the light that is in you is darkness, how great is that darkness." (Matthew 6:23 NKJV)

The fact is darkness cannot overcome light. So if the world is very dark—that means the light is not shining very brightly. If the light is on in a building (the house, *you*), enough darkness cannot be imported to extinguish that light. Darkness only invades what has been vacated by *light*.

If you live in America, you *have been* influenced by this now highly organized and well-orchestrated philosophy of the different gospel. The term given to it by the signers of the *Humanist Manifesto* in 1933 is "Secular Humanism." "Secular" meaning "here and now, earthbound." "Humanism" meaning "centered on humans, human opinion, human experience."

Why should any Christian care about the *Humanist Manifesto?* Only because there is a good possibility that it *is* the spirit of the world and is now in such a total nature as to affect every aspect of the church, especially in the Western World.

I think this is a good place to make the statement—and we will reiterate it down the line—**the Carnal Mind is the Mind of Secular Humanism**. They are "shared brains."

When I use the scripture in Colossians 2:8, the general mindset of listeners (believers) is "but I don't study philosophy."

"Beware, lest any man spoil you through philosophy and vain deceit, after the tradition of men, after the rudiments of the world, and not after Christ." (Colossians 2:8 KJV)

The Amplified Bible makes this clearer: for "spoil you" it uses "make you captive." For philosophy, it states "intellectualism and vain deceit, following human tradition, men's ideas of the material rather than the spiritual world, just crude teachings following the elemental teachings of the universe (life force) and *disregarding* the teachings of Christ the Messiah."

That is our first big mistake—you don't have to "study" philosophy to be affected by it. In fact, philosophy is most powerful when it is "embodied"—lived out rather than if only taught by rote.

Likewise, the Gospel is most powerful when it is "embodied"—lived out, rather than just gaining mental knowledge. I might also mention that *any* creed or religion is most powerful when fully embraced and embodied. This can cast light on why some of those creeds and religions seem to be spreading more rapidly than the Gospel of the Kingdom, because of followers who radically embrace and embody beliefs, right or wrong.

I seriously doubt if many believers in Christ have read the books of the leaders of the secular humanism movement—or attended their conferences. But subliminal (below the level of conscious thinking but strong enough to affect behavior and thinking) affect is real. The strongest value system that prevails in any culture will subliminally affect *anyone in that culture (especially the young)* unless they are consciously aware of that value system and have a *stronger, inner value system.*

Here are some of the reasons why I say that you *have been* influenced by the different gospel:

1. Secular Humanism, simply stated, puts *Man* at the CENTER of life. Life for the humanist is *all about* what the individual wants, feels, thinks, believes, and experiences. Just as "Christians" come in varying degrees of discipleship, so do humanists.

But that is part of the precept—it is all about you, and it is "irrelevant" what anyone else thinks, unless *you* care what they think.

2. To expound on the above, while everyone gets really agitated over the word "atheist"—that term is just a subtopic of "humanist." All of the "-isms" of the world are subtopics to the Central Idea—the autonomy (self-rule) of Man. Man is at the Center. Keep in mind we are taught scripturally that being a Christian means *God* (*Elohim*) is at the Center. So the two (again) main "philosophies" are "Theism" (God at the center)—or "Humanism" (man at the center.) If you think about it, whoever is at the "center" really *is* God, right?

3. The reason I say that if you participated in the Government Education Program in the last fifty years in the U.S., you have been taught, and actually discipled, by humanism, can be seen in the origin of our educational system. The discipling has become extremely pervasive in the last two or three decades, but the teaching, the philosophy, has been in our textbooks for over fifty years.

Of course it started a little at a time, having to not be overly aggressive against Judeo-Christian values that were a part of American heritage. The effect has been slow and subtle, like the frog sitting in lukewarm water, not recognizing that the heat was rising and it was being cooked! But we all know that now in America, the institutions of higher education are all-out "liberal" (the acceptable term) and very openly *anti*-Christian. This is in spite of the fact that there are thousands of teachers who are Christian in the system, doing the best they can to stem the tide.

Two of the most famous names in education in America are Horace Mann and John Dewey.

Horace Mann, called the Father of American Education, is the person credited with starting government-run education in the United States in 1839. He learned his techniques from Prussia, and his motivation was to end education by Christians. He was a Unitarian and did not believe in the inspiration of the Bible or the Trinity. His religion was "secularism." He visualized a world of virtual utopia if he could just eliminate Christianity out of education. He actually allowed that the Bible could be *used* in classrooms, but only for the purpose of teaching morals (tree of knowledge of good and evil)—the doctrine of salvation could not be taught. This is very similar to many eastern religions who see Jesus as a good teacher, but not God. Mann wasn't a signer of the *First Humanist Manifesto*, as that was done in 1933 and he wasn't alive.

However, John Dewey *was* a signer of the *First Humanist Manifesto*. This manifesto talks of a new religion and refers to humanism as a religious movement intended to transcend and replace previous, deity-based systems. Dewey was a leader of the Progressive movement in U.S. education. He grabbed the torch of educational reform and principles of education from Mann and helped to establish them. It's taken a few years, but they have pretty much succeeded in reaching that goal!

In fact, in 1961, our Supreme Court in *Torcaso v. Watkins* ruled that Secular Humanism *is* a religion—so all the talk about "keeping religion" out of the classroom, the separation of church and state, means only the principles of one religion can be taught—the one that underlies all government education: Secular Humanism.

On behalf of all those dedicated believers who have given themselves to teaching in the midst of this system, they are the lights in the darkness and, of course, a blessing. None of this is intended to disparage them. But they are greatly overruled, and the teachers I talk with know that. They are sweeping back the ocean.

So now, on to some of the "finer values" that Secular Humanism has imparted to us, our children, and our grandchildren; the following are some quotes from well-known humanists and their manifestos:

- "We do not believe in a prayer-answering God; no God will save us; we must save ourselves."
- "We believe in the good life, here and now."
- "We believe in personal peace and affluence."

Aside from direct quotes, their statements of faith include belief in "autonomy," meaning they do not believe that man answers to anyone but himself. Of course not. If you don't believe there is a supernatural God, then who would you answer to, besides yourself?

They believe that ethics are "situational, relative"—in other words there are *no absolutes*. Of course not, if there is no supernatural God. So what is "ethical and moral" is totally subject to how you feel, what you think, and what outcome you would like to have in a situation.

I think this means they don't believe in *truth*. So "lies" really aren't "lies"—because a lie can only be in contrast to **Truth**.

Then the same system, when it's failing, because it really promotes anarchy, protests with books like *The Age of Entitlement and Narcissism*, wondering how this all happened! I guess it "just happened," kinda like the Big Bang!

By now you have probably noticed some similarities between the influence of Secular Humanism on our culture and the "issues" of beloved believers, hopefully starting with yourself. The highly "individualistic" thinking that is promoted by Secular Humanism is, of itself, the Trojan Horse for the younger generation. "They promise them liberty, when they themselves are the slaves of depravity..." (2 Peter 2:19 AMP)

The church is as fragmented as society, and why wouldn't we be, having drunk of the poison of the original lie? And each succeeding generation sinks a little lower in the "individualistic" thinking, becoming more lukewarm and passive about anything outside their own concern.

I can hear someone protesting now about all the "good works" that the church does, as if to justify one's position. But keep in mind the definition of "good" comes from the Tree of Knowledge of "Good and Evil." Even Horace Mann didn't mind the Bible being used, as long as it was about morals and "good" behavior!

Remember, the Carnal Mind is the Mind of Secular Humanism; both are CENTERED on the "good life, here and now" and "personal peace and affluence." They share brains.

8
THE LUKEWARM CHURCH

At the risk of repeating myself, this *is* relevant to us. The church at large has been conditioned and desensitized to the point of tolerance and passivity—individually and corporately—to this totally antichrist influence. And it manifests in the Body of Christ as "the different gospel"—more man-conscious, man-centered than God-conscious. It manifests because it appeals to our flesh and what we consider to be the "blessings" of God.

God, indeed, is a Blesser. But that is quite different than making the "good life, here and now" our reason for living.

The seventh church addressed in the Book of Revelation, Laodicea, is looking more like it could be talking to us today, the lukewarm, frog-in-the-water, need of nothing church (note the "*you* say..." part)—but in reality we are poor, wretched, and naked, wearing the clothing of religion but perhaps looking a lot like the emperor who, in reality, had *no* clothes.

Even the name of the church, Laodicea, ties the different gospel Paul spoke of with Secular Humanism. A contemporary definition from the two root words that make up the word Laodicea means "the opinion of people." Hmmm, like maybe we should consider what the *people* think—and not be so concerned about what the *Bible* says...

My husband had an experience that seemed somewhat laughable at the time, but was very serious. He was a member of the board of a young and prosperous, scripturally based church. A discussion was going on about decisions to be made. Differing ideas and opinions were being expressed. One member of the board commented, "this is what the Bible says." An elder board member, who had seemed to be sleeping through most of the discussion, came awake and said, "I don't care what the Bible says, this is the way we are going to do it!"

And so it was, because he was influential in many ways and others didn't want to go contrary to his opinion. The opinion of the people: man-centered, don't rock the boat, don't make any waves. I read a local church sign that said, "Love doesn't make waves." *Seriously?? Who forgot to tell Jesus and Paul... speaking the Truth, in love?*

Many churches today are very concerned about trying to meet the needs of people or keeping people happy with more programs. Not only is this man-centered gospel not recognized in the church, but it is not effective either! There will always be another need, and there will always be someone better at meeting "needs." If our goal is simply "meeting the needs," we will be absorbed with those needs to the neglect of the very purpose of the existence of the church. Jesus said, "Seek ye first the kingdom of God and His righteousness, and all these things will be added to you." (Matthew 6:33) First means FIRST... nothing before it!

I heard the Spirit say, "Secular Humanism is to one's belief system what chemotherapy is to one's natural immune system: it has the power to wipe it out, while providing temporary benefits."

The subliminal effect of Secular Humanism is the unrecognized, undiscerned source of the double-mindedness of a very weak body of Christ.

"The desires of the flesh are opposed to the Holy Spirit and the desires of the Spirit are opposed to the flesh (entire nature of man without the Holy Spirit), for these are antagonistic to each other, so that you are prevented from doing what you desire to do." (Galatians 5:17 AMP)

This scripture sounds like we can function from one or the other, but not both. Either the carnal mind and nature of man will prevail and prevent the Spirit; or the Spirit will prevail and prevent the carnal mind.

Again, the overwhelming influence of Humanism and its disguised agenda for exercising dominion over mankind has propagated some type of "tolerance"—using accusations that if we as believers are bold about our beliefs and our walk with God, we are bigots, biased and unloving. And there is never an end to what we are to tolerate, and eventually accept or even embrace, to *please men*, meaning the carnal nature of man with its carnal mind.

Paul clearly stated in his teachings that "Pleasing Men" was what he was referring to as the different gospel, and it comes from a different spirit, and it requires a modified or a different Jesus.

"I have come in My Father's name and with His power, and you do not receive Me (fully); but if *another* comes in his own name and his own power (man) and with no authority but himself, you will receive him and give him your approval." (John 5:43 AMP)

Verse 44, "How is it possible for you to *believe*, you who are content to seek and receive praise and honor and glory from one another, and yet do not seek the praise and honor and glory which comes from *Him* who alone is God?"

"And yet many even of the leading men believed and trusted in Him. But because of the Pharisees they did not confess it, for fear that they would be expelled from the synagogue." (John 12:42 AMP)

Verse 43, "For they loved the approval and the praise and the glory that comes from men more than the glory that comes from God. (They valued their credit with men more than their credit with God.)"

God only has one competitor today—MAN. Jesus legally won back the jurisdiction that was given to satan through Adam, and through the new birth, the Body of Christ has now become the one who can exercise righteous, legitimate authority in the earth. But the neglect of that authority creates a vacuum that the powers of darkness will gladly fill.

9

SYNCRETISM

So now back to what started this conversation, Colossians 2:8 from the Amplified Version: "See to it that no one carries you off as spoil or makes you captive by his so-called philosophy and intellectualism and vain deceit, following human tradition (men's ideas of the material rather than the spiritual world) just crude notions following the rudimentary and elemental teachings of the universe and disregarding (the teachings of) Christ the Messiah."

If we could grasp the essence of this scripture, we would be well on our way to understanding 1) the carnal mind and 2) the different gospel. To be sure, we need what Paul speaks of in 1 Corinthians 14:7-8 AMP: "If even inanimate musical instruments, such as the flute or the harp, do not give distinct notes, how will anyone know or understand what is played? And if the war bugle gives us an uncertain, indistinct call, who will prepare for battle?"

In the military, a soldier must know the bugle calls, the difference in revelry and taps. The different sounds of the shofar were used to alert the people of God to different events and elicit different responses. How can the great body of believers, the Body of Christ, arise, if there is no clear distinction between what is the "carnal mind" and the "mind of the spirit"? From the writings of Paul in Romans and Corinthians, he seemed to be convinced that this was no minor theme.

Let's take another look at Colossians 2:8 from the Amplified version. It is important to grasp the thoughts in "vain philosophy," "vain deceit," and "tradition of men." In place of "beware," the Amplified version uses the phrase "see to it," a little stronger statement. "See to it that no one carries you off as spoil or makes you captive…" Much stronger than "beware that no one spoil you."

"To the victor goes the spoils"—we understand this term used in the Old Testament. The person who won got to take the "captives" and their stuff! It seems that little notice has been taken of this important passage. He is warning us of the power of *philosophy and tradition* to take us "captive." And along with that goes all our stuff! He is actually warning us of the power of thought, especially subliminal thought.

I used to think "subliminal" was only about advertising—secret, hidden images (messages to the mind). But it's actually the sum of the message of the culture in which you live!

We are familiar with the passage in 2 Corinthians 10:5 AMP: "CASTING DOWN imaginations and every high thing that exalts itself against the knowledge of God, bringing every thought into captivity to the obedience of Christ." I think we would be on solid ground to say that the thoughts that we do not "take captive" will end up taking *us* captive.

Subliminal messages affect our thoughts. They are probably the "source" of some of those thoughts when you ask yourself, "Where did *that* come from?"

Of course, this has been highly developed in the world of technology today. "Thought" is everything. That makes knowing *truth* personally so much more essential to the one who wants to live in a manner that overcomes the world!

The Old Testament is filled with wars fought on a natural battleground with actual weapons, blood, etc. But Paul is speaking of a different warfare, not with flesh and blood and actual weapons, but one more powerful because it is so well disguised.

In reference to the words "vain philosophy" (KJV) Amplified uses "so-called philosophy and intellectualism," *following human tradition (men's ideas of the material rather than the spiritual world)*. This is a very good one-line description of Secular Humanism to which we should give attention. Remember, Paul is warning us of the power in this philosophy and human tradition to captivate us.

I realize believers take various positions on whether we can be "taken captive." Some don't believe anything from the evil one can touch a believer, whether by demons or other methods. Some give demons more power than they have in the life of a believer. But I'm not talking about demons possessing you, and Paul wasn't either.

Second Timothy 2:25-26 talks about a situation wherein one may be taken captive, and Verse 25 offers deliverance to those who "oppose themselves" (work against themselves.) We are all in that group from time to time.

The offer is that if, through hearing the instruction of the Word, they would *repent* and come to *know* and *acknowledge* the Truth, they can "recover themselves" out of the snare of the devil, after being taken captive by him at his will. (AMP: "being held captive by him.")

We do not believe that the devil can march into a believer's life and just take over. In reality, he is a defeated foe, being made so by Jesus' victory. So there must be some inroad, some means by which the devil gets an opportunity.

Again, Paul is connecting this captivity with the measure of Truth that is influencing your life. "Oppose themselves" and "recover themselves" sound like something self-inflicted.

Now to finish up on Colossians 2:8. In the KJV, "following the tradition of men after the rudiments of the world." The Amplified says, "following human tradition—men's ideas of the material rather than the spiritual world—just crude notions following the rudimentary and elemental teachings of the universe, and disregarding the teachings of Christ the Messiah."

Some people would call this radical. Paul says the teachings of the natural, material universe are elemental (elementary, basic), and this is what he is warning us about. All the so-called intellectualism, sense, and reason to the highest power of the human ability has the power to take you, the believer, captive by deception. This influence has the power to "draw one away" from the teachings of Christ to such a place that they are no longer functioning as a supernatural, born again believer, but living as "mere men," how Paul addressed the carnal Christians of Corinth.

Do we see again the "twos"? It isn't the natural world, the universe that God created, that is at war with Him. It is the *philosophy* of natural man, rejecting Truth, and then actually subjecting all creation to their self-imposed curse that comes with "trusting in the arm of flesh."

My question is: How will we see to it that we are not taken captive if we do not recognize the strategy of the enemy?

The prophet Elijah addressed this very clearly as recorded in 1 Kings 18:21 AMP: "Elijah came near to all the people and said, How long will you halt and limp between two opinions? If the Lord is God, follow Him! But if Baal, then follow him."

The word "opinions" carries the meaning of "syncretism" (trying to merge two differing and opposing thoughts.) The prophets obviously had become so deceived that they thought they could serve *both* God and Baal. Something had happened to their minds!

My paraphrase of Micah 3:11-12 is this: Zion's leaders would judge for a bribe, the priests would teach for hire, and the prophets would divine for money. But they would still "lean on the Lord and say, Is not the Lord among us? No evil can come upon us."

The prophet Micah told them that Zion would be plowed like a field and Jerusalem would become heaps of ruins because of them, because of the syncretism, trying to blend two opposing doctrines. Of course, what the prophet said, happened. Syncretism is trying to blend two opposing thoughts, the "mind of the flesh" and the "mind of the spirit."

Suffice it to say from James 1:7: "Let not the double-minded man think that he will receive anything from the Lord."

10

THE WORD OF GOD

I would like to think that some of these passages would affect you like they do me. I think they are scary. Maybe that is a "fear of the Lord" response. Having been saved at the age of fourteen, receiving Holy Spirit Baptism at the age of fifteen, and being a student of the Word for many years, it is scary to me to think that **I can invalidate the power of the Word in my own life**.

It doesn't matter how long I have studied, how much scripture I know and can quote, how many miracles or healings we have witnessed. For those of us who *do* believe that the Bible is the inspired and inerrant Word of God, we also need to know that we can "invalidate" the Word's operation in our own lives.

Jesus said in John 6:63 KJV: "The words that I speak unto you are spirit and they are life."

Hebrews 4:12 states that the Word of God is quick (alive.) I depend on the Word of God to be a quickening to my spirit and to work powerfully in my life. So what could possibly stop the Word from doing so in me? Let's go to the scriptures.

"So for the sake of your tradition (the rules handed down by your forefathers), you have set aside the Word of God (depriving it of force and authority and making it of no effect.)" (Matthew 15:6 AMP)

The Lord went on to state that they drew near to Him with their mouths and honored Him with their lips, but their hearts were far from Him. He was expounding on the previous statement—no matter what they said or quoted, if their actions and decisions didn't match up, they were elevating the tradition of man *above* the Word of God. Again, Traditions of Men verses the Word of God (twos.)

Verse 9 says, "Uselessly do they worship Me, for they teach as doctrines the commands of man."

Mark 7:13 AMP puts it this way, "Thus you are nullifying and making void and of no effect (the authority of) the Word of God through your tradition, which you (in turn) *hand on*."

Nullifying, making void, depriving of force and authority, making of no effect. These are strong statements about elevating the carnal mind of man above the mind of God, His thoughts, His ways.

The absolute infallibility of God's Word is stated in Isaiah 55:11 KJV: "So shall my word be that goeth forth out of my mouth: it shall not return unto me void, but it shall accomplish that which I please, and it shall prosper in the thing whereto I sent it."

The position of authority we give to the Word of God in our own lives determines whether it will "prosper in the thing whereto I sent it."

The Lord was talking about seed being sown into the ground and producing fruit. The Word of God is "seed" containing the Life of God. All natural seed has life in it, else it wouldn't do any good to plant it in the ground. You plant a seed to bring forth more fruit than the one seed planted.

"You have been born again not from a mortal origin (seed, sperm) but from one that is immortal by the ever living and lasting Word of God." (1 Peter 1:23 AMP)

Mark 4 speaks at length about the "seed" of the Word of God. The parable is the Sower sowing Seed, explaining that the "seed" is the Word of God, and the "ground" in which the seed is sown is the heart. That is very important.

In Mark 4:11, Jesus told His disciples He was speaking about the Kingdom of God. In Verse 13, He asks if they understood the parable. Then He asked, "How then is it possible for you to discern and understand all the parables (regarding the Kingdom), if you don't understand this one." That makes this chapter of the Bible pretty important—it is key to understanding the other parables and teachings of the Kingdom of God.

In this parable, it is always important to remember that it is about the eternal, incorruptible seed, the Word of God, and the ground, the heart of man. Several scenarios are discussed. In the first one, the Word is stolen before it ever reaches the heart, yielding no fruit.

In the second one, it is received with joy (into the heart), but it never stays long enough to get rooted. The parable is that these endure for a little while, but when trouble or persecution arises because of the Word, they are offended, become displeased, indignant, resentful, and they stumble and fall away.

What is at issue here is the Word; it is the reason for the persecution/ trouble. And the persecution and trouble are the reason for the offense and falling away. No endurance, no fruit. In other words, if there is any waiting, perseverance or opposition involved, I have no desire to participate. It's called "casting away your confidence." The thief comes immediately to steal the Word.

In the third one, the seed goes into the ground (heart) but there are also thorns. The thorns are identified as "cares of this world, deceitfulness of riches, and lusts of other things entering in" (to the heart) which choke the Word and it becomes unfruitful.

In the fourth one, the seed sown on good ground bears fruit thirty times, sixty times, even as much as a hundred times. The *seed* wasn't the issue; the *ground* (heart) was the issue. The Word in the heart had to be watched over, cared for, and kept free from other things "entering in" so as not to choke the Word and cause it to be unfruitful. Proverbs 4:23, "Guard your heart with all diligence..."

"And we also thank God continually for this—that when you received the message of God from us, you welcomed it not as the word of mere men, but as it truly is, the Word of God, which is effectually at work in you who believe (exercising its superhuman power in those who adhere to, trust in, and rely on it.)" (1 Thessalonians 2:13 AMP)

How important is the Word? The Word is *alive.* (Hebrews 4:12) Satan comes immediately to *steal* the Word. (Mark 4:15) The *war* is over the Word. In the beginning was the Word and the Word was with God and the Word *was* God. (John 1:1) And the title by which He is called is *"the WORD of GOD."* (Revelation 19:13)

PART 3

THE WAR BETWEEN
THE CARNAL MIND AND THE SPIRIT

11

OLD WINE, NEW WINE

"Who will release and deliver me from this body of death?" (Romans 7:24 AMP)

"For the desires of the flesh are opposed to the Spirit, and the desires of the Spirit are opposed to the flesh; for they are antagonistic to each other, (continually withstanding and in conflict with each other.)" (Galatians 5:17 AMP)

"For the law of the Spirit of life in Christ Jesus (law of our new being) has freed me from the law of sin and death." (Romans 8:2 AMP)

Summarizing up to this point, we have focused on the conflict, perhaps outright war, between the influence and effect of sense and reason without Holy Spirit (carnal mind) upon the human mind and heart in contrast to the influence of the Word and Spirit (mind of the Spirit) upon the human mind and heart.

Hopefully it is dawning upon us that the overcoming life Jesus has obtained for us will be experienced by living from the superior realm of the Spirit, the Kingdom of God, and fully relying upon His integrity and power, rather than on the arm of flesh. And that is called a life of faith.

"And no one, after drinking old wine immediately desires new wine, for he says, The old is better." (Luke 5:39 AMP) Jesus was using the wine and wineskin to reveal the change from the old covenant (natural) to the new covenant (spiritual.)

Old Wine—is like our comfortable, satisfying "wine" of what we believe and have somewhat experienced of the Kingdom of God—our present level of faith. We resist the unfamiliar, new insight from Holy Spirit—the lifting of the veil.

In the "dimension of time" there is always an "old" and a "new." Revivalists realize that the "old" or "previous" move of and experience with God *resists* even *persecutes* the present NEW. "...Be established in the **present truth**." (2 Peter 1:12 KJV)

The Old Covenant was given for natural men with the fallen nature. It was to provide them a means of access to the Living God *until* the New Covenant would come. But they were blinded by their tradition (something passed down)—all the experiences and teachings of their ancestors. They were so focused on "earthly life, and an earthly kingdom" they could not even fathom for a moment something so far removed from their paradigm.

But it isn't just the Jews of the Old Covenant that prefer their traditions. It is a characteristic of the carnal nature, which lives from comfort to comfort. Any move of God by the Spirit, any revelation of the Word and Spirit can become tradition—something that we look back upon and become so familiar with that we no longer need the Spirit of God involved with our activities; and we presumptuously just go through the motions, not knowing the "glory has departed."

There are several examples of this in the Word. The Priest Eli: "And she named the child Ichabod, saying, 'The glory is departed from Israel'—because the ark of God had been captured and because of her father-in-law (Eli) and her husband." (1 Samuel 4:21 AMP)

"For those who honor Me I will honor, and those who despise Me shall be lightly esteemed." (1 Samuel 2:30 AMP) Of course, this was referencing Eli's practice of honoring (placing higher) his sons above the Lord.

Samson—not recognizing or wanting to see the subtle influence of Delilah and her motives—gradually fell into the trap of the enemy, and the Word says, "For Samson did not know that the Lord had departed from him." (Judges 16:20 AMP)

The Serpent of Bronze in the Book of Numbers, Chapter 21; the Lord told Moses to make a brazen serpent set on a pole. When he lifted it up for the people to "gaze" at, they were healed of the bites of the serpents. This is all prophetic and foretelling of Christ on the Cross and the healing covenant.

Yet many years later during the reign of King Hezekiah, it was said of him that he did right in the sight of the Lord, according to all that David had done. In addition to removing the high places, breaking the images, and cutting down the Asherim, it is mentioned that he broke in pieces the bronze serpent.

The Israelites had carried the bronze serpent around all those years, *after* the purpose that God ordained had expired, and made an idol of it by burning incense to it. Hezekiah rightly named it as just "a piece of bronze." What God had anointed as a means of receiving healing had become an idol. (2 Kings 18:4)

Under the influence of the carnal mind, we begin to make "formulas" (traditions) out of what the Spirit of God did, in response to faith, in the past. We find "rest" (not being challenged), confidence (self), affirmation (self), and perhaps some pride in the spiritual victories we have experienced.

In His comment about the old and new wine, Jesus could have been speaking to the church today: more focused on the natural, sense-bound life than on the transformational reality of the new nature revealed in the Word of God—the superior reality of the unseen realm of the Spirit.

Paul, addressing the Galatians, in Chapter 3, Verse 1, said in very plain words, "Oh foolish Galatians, who hath bewitched you...?" (KJV)

As so many believers today are more sensitive to themselves than the Spirit, Paul probably would have been ushered out if he had stood up and asked that question in church today! The Amplified version, in its typical style, is even stronger, saying, "O you poor and silly and thoughtless and unreflecting and senseless Galatians! Who has fascinated or bewitched or cast a spell over you?"

Speaking of their "foolishness," the context was the same as with King Asa when the prophet told him he had done "foolishly." Like the prophet to King Asa, Paul was talking about relying on the arm of flesh—rather than relying on God, particularly after the glorious firsthand experiences of the deliverance of God.

Paul asked the question (Verse 3), "Having begun your new life spiritually with the Holy Spirit, are you now reaching perfection by dependence on the flesh?"

The term "bewitched" is very accurate in describing the effect of the carnal mind on a believer; it is very much like a spell. And this is particularly true when you factor in the subliminal effect of the contemporary (meaning joined to the temporary) Christianized culture, the influence that slips in, unaware.

While the Word clearly reveals our victory in Christ—the spoiling of all principalities and powers that would keep mankind in slavery, a salvation that incorporates every form of deliverance and well-being—still a veil seems to be over the spirit of the Church.

The carnal mind carries the power of witchcraft over a believer. Perhaps this could be best understood if we realize that to be introduced to Truth (His Word is Truth)—but not act upon that Truth—is to reject Truth. The effect is blinding.

When we are born again, the "veil" that separates us from Truth is removed. If we neglect or refuse Truth in our lives, the veil returns. Paul also calls this being "seduced." Second Corinthians 4:4 speaks of blinding, a smokescreen, as a result of unbelief.

If you have become aware of the carnal mind and how it works in your life, you have also become aware of how much influence it has over a believer; and that you, trusting in yourself, cannot overthrow it. Flesh cannot overthrow flesh. Jesus said, "What is born of the flesh is flesh. What is born of the spirit is spirit." (John 3:6) One realm is superior and has power and authority over the other.

Many preachers construct their "sermons" around the carnal nature of religious mankind, addressing the wrongs of man's behavior seemingly in an effort to reform them. But what is needed is sufficient revelation from the pulpit to encourage a maturing in believers. Elsewise, we will attempt to subdue the flesh by the power of the flesh, because we won't be enlightened to the power of the Spirit. There may be some temporary results from behavior modification, but ultimately the flesh will fail again. Each time a believer cycles in this manner, discouragement takes another deeper toll till one has no heart to even believe.

12
"That's life..."

As a younger person, I viewed life as most humans do, thinking that people and circumstances were the controlling factors in life, and "That's life..." Of course, that is actually true in our youth. Our outlook on life is largely passed on to us from our family and their worldview. So in my life, that meant a strong poverty outlook, extreme insecurity and consequently somewhat of a depressed view of life and its difficulties.

I grew up in a family of six children which were eventually abandoned by an alcoholic father. When this came to fruition, my mother had never driven a car or worked a day outside of the home. Nevertheless, she undertook to guide and provide for all that her six dependent children needed. With no child support and no state assistance, my mother gave herself to what was needed and consequently instilled a wonderful work ethic in our family. But what stuck in my thinking was that I needed to always work hard and hold on to what I had.

Indeed, reality is that natural life on earth, apart from faith and the truth revealed in the Word of God, is controlled by the natural world of sense, reason and logic. Whoever is best at mastering these natural abilities will control mindsets and people in the earth.

But into my earthly reality stepped Jesus. "I am come that they might have **life** and that they might have it more abundantly." (John 10:10 KJV)

Although I was not raised in a Christian home, I was drawn to the God of the Bible at the age of fourteen through a personal encounter with Holy Spirit. But my experiences with church were dwarfed by a spiritual hunger to know God more personally. I received Holy Spirit baptism a year later. This hunger caused me to search, and gradually begin to find in the Word of God, the keys for which my heart was looking.

Ezekiel 36 speaks of a "new heart" and a "new spirit." This, along with other scriptures, indicates the heart and the spirit are not one and the same. If the heart is the "seat of our affections and desires" as well as where we make choices and decisions from, it is really the control center of our being. On the other hand, it is our spirit that is born again and where Holy Spirit can make His dwelling when invited into the New Nature. But never will Holy Spirit act in the capacity of forcing or coercing one to do anything—anymore than our Father God or Jesus will.

In reference to the assignment of Holy Spirit, Jesus said, "He will show you things to come. He will guide you into all Truth." The one who seeks to coerce and control is the one called our "adversary." We must never confuse the methods of the two kingdoms, light and darkness.

This reveals much about the carnal nature and its origin, for it *does* exert force, coercion, and control with much fear, intimidation and manipulation. It will attempt to influence us in these ways; and if we are influenced, then these same influences will work *through us*, on others... to control, coerce, intimidate and manipulate.

When we are spiritually born again, we receive a new heart too. It is a heart of hunger for knowing our Father and the truth of His Word. If you hunger and thirst for experiencing this relationship with God, you will be filled. (Matthew 7:7 KJV) "ASK, and it shall be given you; SEEK, and ye shall find; KNOCK, and the door will be opened unto you." Hungering, asking, seeking, knocking—all led me to realize the beginnings of fulfillment of my desire to know the Lord.

"For therein (the Gospel) is the righteousness of God revealed from faith to faith, that is, springing from faith and leading to more faith." (Romans 1:17 AMP)

Faith...perceiving as reality what is not revealed to the senses. In the beginning walk of faith, no doubt one takes hold of individual scriptures and promises, praying and believing that as we "look at the things that are unseen," the God of His Word will do what He says He will do. This became our life—my husband and I.

Though the human side of us might be satisfied with God supplying all of our needs with sustaining miracles and healings of every kind, as well as opening doors to minister around the world, our hearts and God's heart aren't satisfied until they are truly joined. That deep inner satisfaction and peace won't come until we are not only claiming and experiencing the promises of God and His Word, but we are *thinking His thoughts* by the Word and living in the realm of the Spirit. That is the realm in which we, as new creations, are created to *live*.

A key revelation for this life is, "For as he (a man) THINKETH—in his heart, *so is he*...." (Proverbs 23:7 KJV—Emphasis Added)

The concept of this scripture can be found in many places in the Word. One that particularly supports this is Proverbs 4:23 AMP: "Keep and guard your *heart* with all vigilance, for out of it flow the springs of life." And Jesus taught that *everything that defiles is coming out of the thinking of the heart.* We must "guard our heart" if we want to receive the thoughts of God's Word and His Spirit—because the heart is also where the influence of the carnal mind will take root.

It is futile, defeating to the believer, and contrary to the Word of God for us to preach against the works of the flesh without addressing the source, the heart. And it is equally as futile to address the defilement of the heart of a believer without teaching him how to access his birthright of righteousness and fill his heart with the thoughts of God, which in turn will change his mental outlook and actions.

The THINKING that takes place in the depth of our inner being, the *heart*, will ultimately direct our mind, and then our actions. The one who is a believer in Jesus Christ is no longer destined to be controlled by natural thinking, that which is the result of our senses interacting with logic and reasoning powers of our mind. Romans 12:2 tells us the unrenewed mind and natural thinking are the reasons we are conformed to this world. There is a *transformation* that can take place by *replacing the source of thoughts.*

13

POSSESSING YOU

According to the Word, *all modes of thinking pass through the heart of man.* It is somewhat of a "clearinghouse" where decisions are made on which modes of thinking one will embrace. It is within the power of the heart of a born again person to embrace or release modes of thought, including those instilled by upbringing or previously embraced in life. Forgiveness, for instance, as found in Luke 6:37 and Matthew 18:35. The principle found in these scriptures is one of "*release.*" If we release, *we will BE released.*

By realizing the decisions regarding modes of thought are taking place in the HEART of MAN, we can distinguish between this reality and the metaphysical mind-over-matter methods of philosophical positive thinking and optimism, as well as the practice of denying natural circumstances.

So far we've realized that thoughts are guiding and defining our lives, howbeit in a slower manner than being influenced from external sources; and much of this is being instilled silently, in a subliminal manner as the result of our culture. Secondly, ultimately the thoughts that endure and guide us are the ones that become "rooted" in our hearts. Thirdly, we can recognize and change, by the ability of a believer to choose, the source of our thoughts: of the spirit or of the flesh.

For anyone who believes the scripture "The just shall live by faith," it will be a foundational truth for living "faith to faith." We can grow the thoughts of God in our heart, just as you can grow seed in a garden. This, in turn, will renew your mind out of the abundance of the heart.

The reality of the thoughts of God bearing fruit is part of maturing in righteousness and growing in faith. The young and immature in faith will "take hold" only of the individual scriptures they need for their life on earth. Though it is an exercise of faith, the focus is more pragmatic and earthbound than it is "transformational." In many ways, the thinking is still "conformed to this world" as it focuses on our needs.

"The Word has to go *in you* and TAKE POSSESSION of you!" (Winnie Banov)

Do you possess the Word—or does the Word *possess* you? Going from faith to faith, glory to glory, maturing, moves you from only possessing the Word to the Word having possession of you, your heart. His thoughts in your heart are the ones that won't return void but will accomplish what He has sent them forth to do. (Isaiah 55:11)

In Romans 7:17, Paul made reference to the carnal nature which had previously "possessed" him. The Amplified Bible says the "sin principle (nature) was in him, working because it had possession of him." Second Peter 1:4 states that we become partakers of the "divine nature" by means of His precious and exceedingly great promises.

We partake of the Word, the Living Bread. "Man shall not live by bread alone, but by every Word that proceeds out of the mouth of God."

The purpose of salvation is to restore what Adam relinquished in the Garden. He was an "underlord," and he was in total right relationship with God with total access to, and authority over, the Garden. He was made in God's likeness with authority to choose. And we too are "freed" from the carnal nature at the new birth, with the authority and responsibility to choose "whom we will serve."

"Do you not know that if you continually surrender yourselves to anyone to do his will, you are the slaves of him whom you obey, whether that be to sin, which leads to death, or to obedience which leads to righteousness?" (Romans 6:16 AMP)

It is remarkable that this statement would follow the great revelation of identification with Christ in death and resurrection, as if to emphasize that even with all that has been done to give us new life, we still have to walk out a life of faith and obedience to actually possess that life on earth.

Our spirit is born again and we have full access to the riches of God's grace through being justified. (Romans 5:1-2) God doesn't "possess" a person when that person is born again; He makes Himself and abundant life fully available to us, to the degree of "...as He *is*, so are we, in this world." (I John 4:17 AMP) As we continually enter into the abundant life, it fills us—to the point of fullness and possession.

In essence, what we have been given access to is greater than the position of the first Adam as underlord. We are actually *made to be* "*joint heirs*" with Jesus, who was the firstborn of *many* brethren... we are that brethren!

"The assignment of the Holy Spirit in this dispensation is to cause men to obtain and *be governed by* the Holy Spirit." (2 Corinthians 3:8 AMP, paraphrase)

That "governing" doesn't come because God is a taskmaster controlling us. It comes through our desire for relationship with our

Heavenly Father, through loving submission and obedience to His Word and Spirit.

"To move in the ways of the Spirit is to submit our lives to be governed by the Spirit." (Romans 8:4 AMP, paraphrase)

Romans 8:7 reminds us that the mind of the flesh does not, cannot, submit itself to God; it is an enemy of God. To move and live in a way that is possessed by the Word and Spirit of God is to be "free indeed" from the law of sin and death. "Ye shall know the Truth and the Truth shall make you free." (John 8:32 KJV)

14

The Superior Realm of the Spirit

The superior realm of the Spirit is the Kingdom of God. It is important to grasp that living in the realm of the Spirit *is* a life of faith. Likewise, living a life of faith *is* living in the realm of the Spirit. To say it another way, walking after the Spirit is walking by faith; walking by faith is walking after the Spirit.

We (my husband and I) understood this "union" as younger believers. Through a simplicity of devotion to the Lord, we were living in the New Creation Reality. In the past ten years or so, we have frequently heard people comment to us that we are "different" because we "merge the realm of the Spirit with the walk of faith." Apparently to many believers, that isn't the model they have seen, or the teaching they have heard.

Actually, *we* have done *no such* thing. We only understood that the WORD IS SPIRIT from the unseen realm, and that is what FAITH responds to. We only followed what is in the Word, which is our only basis for faith.

People have separated the walk of faith from walking after the Spirit, making them two separate camps. This is not scriptural and certainly not beneficial to the developing of the new creation realities. We find that many in the Body of Christ have very little understanding of this truth.

I believe the only way to grasp the thoughts of God in relation to our total salvation, and what He has prepared for us to enter into and live *even while on earth,* is to approach the Bible as a whole, with an open heart and mind. That means dropping all our carnal and religious understanding at the altar before embarking.

I have experienced at least three different times in my life when the Lord, in response to my seeking His help, has told me to dump everything I thought I knew about Him and the Word. This was before the age of computers and hard drives.

The first time I experienced this was very scary. I had never heard anyone (in church) say that before. Still having the mentality of working hard and holding on, I viewed this instruction through those glasses. I thought, "It has taken me these several years to get where I am—and now you tell me to dump it all?" At this time, we had experienced personal miracles, healings, provisions, operated in spiritual gifts, taught the Word... and now I was to start over?

Thankfully, my relationship with Holy Spirit was such that I could receive comfort and encouragement to obey. So I obeyed. Such a move was quite disorienting to a performance driven person. But the Lord had told me He would "put back in" what was of Him, and that is exactly what He did. In a very short time, I began to know what was clearly Truth—and that Truth was now a foundation to build upon and accelerate.

As I mentioned earlier, I wasn't raised in church. But it didn't take too many years—in church—to pick up a lot of "religious flesh" and be seduced by the "different gospel." So I am eternally grateful to the Lord for this "spiritual intervention," working with me in such a way as to open my eyes, from time to time, to that which was in vain and fruitless, not to mention heavy baggage that slowed and impeded my journey.

No doubt, all of us have fallen into the Galatians error—probably more than once. That error is "Having begun in the Spirit—but reverting back to flesh." Using the scripture—but relying on self. Being laced with the scripture, it is more difficult to recognize; and repentance is even more difficult. But that *is how we recover ourselves out of the snare.* (2 *Timothy* 2:26)

Through many years of endeavoring to walk by faith, walk after the Spirit, we have developed a working definition of how we see this walk:

"Faith is to be influenced, fully persuaded, and won over to the superiority of the realm of the Spirit, the Kingdom of God." Faith is based upon the Word of God.

One effect of what we might call "religious" thinking is that our so-called spiritual lives and our daily lives are separated. There is a disconnect between what we may experience in the wonderful presence of the Lord (assuming you have that) and what we experience in daily life. It is that exact thinking that constitutes the carnal mind of a believer and keeps them projecting all of God's promises to heaven.

"I bear them witness that they have a certain zeal and enthusiasm for God, but it is not enlightened and according to knowledge. For being ignorant of the righteousness that God ascribes and seeking to establish a righteousness of their own, they did not obey or submit themselves to God's righteousness." (Romans 10:2-3 AMP)

Jesus, as recorded in the Gospels, announced and lived the Kingdom of God from the onset of His ministry, confirming that announcement with the signs, wonders and miracles that accompany the preaching of the Gospel of the Kingdom.

"But He said to them, I must preach the Gospel of the kingdom of God to the other cities also, for I was sent for this purpose." (Luke 4:43 AMP)

Much of the church seems to still be struggling with the message and demonstration of the Kingdom of God. Jesus was introducing and demonstrating how the change from the old to the new would look and be different. He was preparing the way for the church, the Body of Christ, to be birthed on the day of Pentecost. And the Book of Acts continued and accelerated that demonstration, as it was now working through the Body of Christ.

When you move past in the Bible, the Gospels and the Book of Acts, you begin to see more fully the transition from the old covenant to the new covenant and the Kingdom of God. But without accepting, embracing and embarking into the Kingdom of God—revelation in the Gospels and the Book of Acts—much of what is known as the Pauline Revelation will literally be "over your head" spiritually and, if anything, become only a mental acceptance. What I mean by that is, you can read the words because they are in your language, but they will not find a place in your heart to grow because there will be a huge disconnect, actually a lack of foundation.

Paul presents the revelation of who God planned, purposed, and destined the born again believers to be—and to do—in the Epistles. It isn't a myth, it isn't allegorical, it isn't a fantasy, and it isn't something that we are to ascribe as a description of heaven after our body dies.

It is actually here and now, existing in the eternal, invisible superior realm of the Spirit. Indeed, it is the revelation of the living Body of Christ in the earth. But a receptiveness and hunger, even a desperation, is needed to leave the old, religious system behind and move into the new, even though the new has been available on earth for some 2,000 years.

Jesus was still speaking to "sense-ruled" people in the Gospels. He couldn't actually tell them about the "new life" until they experienced the "new birth." The whole objective of Jesus, as recorded in the Gospels, was to bring the Jews to believe that Jesus is the Christ. Very little is even hinted at of the completed work of Christ or of the Body of Christ.

"And many other signs truly did Jesus in the presence of his disciples which are not written in this book. But these are written, that ye might believe that Jesus is the Christ, the Son of God; and that believing ye might have life through his name." (John 20:30-31 AMP)

Much of the church still lives in the Gospels, yet not believing that He brought His Kingdom (in the spirit) to earth and demonstrated that Kingdom by His signs.

"The Spirit of the Lord is upon Me, because He has anointed Me to preach good news to the poor; He has sent Me to announce release to the captives and recovery of sight to the blind, *to send forth as delivered those who are oppressed (who are downtrodden, bruised, crushed and broken down by calamity), to proclaim the acceptable year of the Lord (the day when salvation and the free favors of God profusely abound.)*" (Luke 4:18-19 AMP)

Some things to note here:

- Jesus wasn't announcing a chronological time frame—a calendar year. The reference is made to the "year of Jubilee"—also known as the "Acceptable Year of the Lord" in the Old Testament. This was a "year" that happened every 50 years, when those who were enslaved for their unpaid debts were again freed and the properties returned to them. A year of "acceptance" by God.

- The parallel of the natural (Old Covenant) and spiritual (New Covenant) gives the same deliverance, but goes further into the inner man where true freedom and acceptance is experienced.

- There was NO EXPIRATION DATE set on this announcement; it was now eternally declared for whosoever will, whosoever believes and enters in. This release, this deliverance is NOW available to whosoever will.

Jesus was announcing that *He* was the fulfillment of the law of sin and death and had set free eternally all who would believe and receive Him. "But to as many as received him, to them gave he power to become the sons of God, even to them that believe on his name." (John 1:12 KJV)

The Old Covenant believers looked forward to the Kingdom of God, based on promise. But we must know that under the New Covenant, the word "promise" isn't speaking of the future. In fact, the word "promise" in the New Covenant means: "Announcement of a *Gift Given* and consequently to be acknowledged, received, appropriated."

But you might ask, "I believe the Bible to be true—so why aren't the promises coming to me?"

Firstly, the Bible says, "It is of faith, that it might be by grace." There is a lot of teaching today about the topic of "grace." Nothing can take away from the awesome completeness of the grace of God. It is everything we are talking about. But it is a mistake to teach *grace* without teaching *faith*.

"For it is by grace that you are saved, through faith…" (Ephesians 2:8 AMP)

"Inheriting the promise is the outcome of faith in order that it might be given as an act of grace." (Romans 4:16 paraphrase)

"Through Him we have access by faith into this grace, wherein we stand." (Romans 5:2 AMP)

All that is "given by grace" is "received by faith," so how important is faith? We must know that FAITH cannot work with the carnal mind—cannot work with the control we want to exert over circumstances—even after we pray and ask God to work. Whether we understand it or not, we cannot combine the methods of darkness and the flesh with that which is of the spirit and faith.

Bible Faith is this: "Since we consider and look not to the things that are seen but to the things that are unseen; for the things that are visible are temporal, subject to change, but the things that are invisible are eternal and everlasting." (2 Corinthians 4:18 AMP)

You see the connection between faith and the spirit realm. We know what is in the "invisible" realm by the Word and Spirit of God.

15

WALKING IN FAITH

Here is Faith 101: "Be not anxious...don't worry about anything, pray about everything." (Philippians 4:6 paraphrase) I say this is Faith 101 because most people don't even realize that they "pray" about something and then set out to fix or control what they prayed about. That is an exercise in religious futility. Don't bother to pray; it is only making you feel better about yourself, but it *isn't* helping the situation. This is the "Galatians Error"—starting in the Spirit but reverting to the flesh—using scripture but relying on ourselves.

You cannot combine control, manipulation, intimidation, fear (all of the carnal mind and nature) with faith and the Spirit. They won't mix. *Faith relies on the Word of God and the superior realm of the Spirit.*

The Word tells us in Hebrews 4 that the children of Israel didn't enter the Promised Land because they didn't "mix faith with the message." (I think this is the only actual mix that God is pleased with—FAITH with the MESSAGE, His Word.) Mixing faith with the message is what is called "appropriation."

Hebrews 4:6 (AMP) says that even though the works were *prepared* and *waiting* from the foundation of the world, the children of Israel *failed to appropriate it* and did not enter because of unbelief and disobedience.

It is the same today because that chapter is about the "Prepared Rest" that is even now awaiting to be appropriated by the sons of God. This doesn't speak of inactivity or passivity; it speaks of living a life that is completely reliant on the Lord, having repented from the dead works of the carnal mind.

To appropriate means to "personalize, receive, make your own." To respond to the finished work, the gift given, even to "claim" it. Many people have rejected faith and the necessity of appropriating the Word of God because of what came to be called the "name it and claim it gospel." But "claiming" what God has *given* is scriptural.

Sometimes the cycles and seasons that move around the Body of Christ do get into error, leaning too far one way or another. Unfortunately, much valid truth gets thrown out over someone's imbalance, rather than finding the truth and using the Word of God, the sword of the Spirit, to divide and discern.

The "name it/claim it" cycle was a little misuse of the truth of appropriation. But regardless of abuse and misuse, appropriation is the way we receive into our lives that which has been given. And the Word of God abides forever.

In reality, the announcement of the "Gift Given" is for the same purpose as it would be in natural life. It is no different than if, for whatever reason, a potential college student received notification that he had been "given" a scholarship or grant. It is for the purpose of the student responding, actually moving to take possession of the "gift given."

I believe this subject reveals the absolute necessity of a believer to participate in a "growing, maturing" process. There is a growing, maturing process for the sons of God, even as there is a growing, maturing process for natural sons.

I understand through Bible scholars that there are three to five different words from the Greek translated as "sons." You see some of this in the book of 1 John. My understanding is that just as surely as the newborn baby is truly a "son"—there is a vast difference in relationship with the infant son than with the hopefully more mature "son" that is thirty years old.

Clarity comes here from Romans 8:14 (paraphrase): "Those who are led (governed) by the Spirit of God, by the new nature of the inner man, are the (mature) sons of God." Much could be said here, but certainly the thought of being "governed" by the inner, not the outer, is key—whether the "outer" is good spiritual mentoring, or whether the outer is the carnal mind. The measure of maturity is the inner governing of a believer by the Spirit and the Word. And, of course, good spiritual mentoring is vital to maturing as a son of God.

We have experienced supernatural healings and miracles personally for many years. But the last fifteen years, this has increased dramatically. We have several albums in our small congregation of numerous healings and miracles because we develop the culture of the Kingdom and teach the Word, Faith and the Spirit.

The miracles, signs and wonders have increased in many places during the last two decades. We used to think that all we needed was more of the supernatural and more people would become born again. But that isn't necessarily true; just as the children of Israel seemed to "forget" about the miracles and power shown on their behalf, so it is today.

So even though it could and should be a stepping stone in spiritual maturity, the supernatural doesn't affect everyone the same, meaning it doesn't touch the inner man deeply. After all that the children of Israel experienced of miraculous deliverance, miraculous provision, miraculous healings, miraculous guidance, Hebrews 3:12 says they had an evil heart of unbelief, leading them to depart (stand aloof) from the living God. The "aloofness" is indicative of the church today.

In our congregation, we intentionally endeavor to bring our children and youth into experiencing God in a supernatural way. A few years back, our four-year-old grandson, while playing, noticed something on my husband's face and asked what it was. My husband, in his typical joking manner, made light of it; but the grandson said, "That isn't the Kingdom, I'll pray for it!" And he did!

He literally slapped his hand on a mole on my husband's face and cursed it in the name of Jesus. It started drying up, and we later found from a biopsy that it had been cancerous but was now dying. He did the same for his dad a few days later, and a mole on his face dropped off.

Our family doctor said, "You must have been doing some tall praying about that." (He's a believing Catholic). My husband responded, "Not really, let me tell you about it." He told the doctor how the miracle happened; the doctor slipped the report into the file and said, "Here it is if you ever want it."

But the same grandson still had to mature as an individual and grow physically, emotionally and spiritually, going through disciplines and correction to bring him to maturity. Miracles are *not* the Mark of Maturity. Learning to walk by faith, being governed by the Spirit, is the scriptural mark of maturity.

It is time for an apostolic generation of leaders to rise up who will live in such a way, by faith from the Spirit, that they will *pave the way* for the youth who are, and will be experiencing, the supernatural, and be mentors to them.

Galatians 4:1 is speaking of the Jewish tradition, but it's there also for our spiritual application. It simply says that as long as the heir is a child, he does not differ from a slave, even though he is *legally master of all*. But he remains under guardians and trustees. In other words, he never comes into his experiential inheritance, even though he has a legal inheritance, until he fulfills what is the *measure of maturity*, being governed by the Spirit.

So this is where we must apply the New Testament scriptures to understand Spiritual Maturity. We have mentioned several references—1 Corinthians 3:1-3 being very clear about what is and what isn't the measure of maturity. It is all based upon how fully you respond and walk in the superior realm of the Spirit, regardless of whether you operate in spiritual giftings, prophetic, healings, etc.

While stating that the Corinthian Church didn't fall behind in any spiritual gifts, Paul addressed the Corinthians as infants, mere men, under the control of ordinary impulses. How would he address the church today?

But I also want to mention Hebrews 5:11-14, specifically Verses 13 and 14, which define maturity or "full grown men." The criteria here is that one becomes experienced, trained and skilled in the Word of Righteousness. By faith, one can live in right relationship with the Lord to the place that our "senses" become trained "by use" to discern what is good and evil.

Our righteousness is "by faith" so this is speaking of bringing our senses into subjection to faith that "by reason of use," the senses begin to cooperate with your spirit. Here is a "heavy revvy": The *senses* are not to RULE. They are to be TRAINED, by *using*, experiencing the faith walk, to *cooperate*, with the Spirit! Paul said by now, we should be moving on past the warm, fuzzy milk of the Christianized culture that so appeals to our senses....to some level of spiritual maturity.

Understanding that it is the senses working with our logic and reason that form the carnal mind, we can see how important this overlooked scripture is. The *untrained* senses will do what they do... communicate impulses to the brain, which functions by reasoning and logic—the carnal mind.

Anyone who has endeavored to walk by faith, after the Spirit, understands that it is the strong influence of the senses, working with reason and logic, that create the opposition described in Galatians 5:17: the flesh and the spirit at war.

This really sums up what a walk and faith in the Spirit is about. No longer are the senses, coupled with logic and reason, dominating the believer. But the believer, through his walk of faith, has been so affected that the heart, working by the influence of the Spirit, affects and renews the mind, bringing the senses into a place of working and cooperating with the Spirit. And your senses will love it and thank you for it!

By contrast, Hebrews 5:11-12 give an all-too-familiar assessment of much of the Body of Christ. Many have become dull and sluggish in spiritual hearing and insight.

The result is that even though "by the time" we should be teaching others, we still continually need someone to build the basics of faith in our lives, constantly reassuring us of God's love and faithfulness.

The Body of Christ is immature because we have not embarked on the walk of faith, a process by which our senses will become exercised, trained and skilled in the Word of Righteousness.

My assessment is that if we would become aware of the "Galatians error"—and more willing to repent and acknowledge TRUTH, this condition could be quickly reversed.

All creation is groaning for the manifestation of the (mature) sons of God!

16

SEASONS OF CORRECTION

Now we will look at Hebrews, Chapter 12, starting with the promise of Verse 11 that states the seasons of correction will bring the "peaceable fruit of righteousness." Another "heavy revvy": *embarking on the walk of faith is embarking into seasons of correction... for which we praise the Lord!*

As mentioned previously, we have been living in a culture which has been slowly permeated with Humanism for some fifty years. That in itself wouldn't be so impacting if Humanism had not had such an eroding effect on our basic Christian beliefs. But there is one startling attitude in today's church that is so foundational as to affect everything else.

It is the effect of the humanistic thought of "autonomy, self-rule, individualistic thought and action" in place of authority. As the Word says, each man doing what is right in his own eyes.

As we write this, the Supreme Court of the United States has not long ago mandated that all states must legally recognize and grant marriage to same sex couples. What a slap in the face of the church, and it truly smarts.

However, one of the Ten Commandments (I know we don't live *under* the Commandments, but we do live under the *Spirit* of the Commandments)—"Thou shall not commit adultery"—is hardly blinked at by the contemporary (meaning even faith- and Spirit-filled) congregation!

It is all too frequent that another pastor is exposed as being involved in adultery; and of course, that means another commandment about bearing false witness has been violated also. *And where are the people who stand and protest about those behaviors?* The carnal, religious mind, while showing a little indignation, has said, "Well, that's not *quite* as bad, maybe understandable, justifiable..."

I absolutely accept all the scriptures—and absolutely disagree with this recent ruling—but we must keep this in mind: despite the presence of same sex relationships in the cities of Sodom and Gomorrah, the Word says it was the "absence of righteousness," not the "presence of homosexuality," that brought the destruction of these cities. I am simply calling out the hypocrisy of the church that claims to be so devoted to the Bible, but it is *selective* devotion. It is the carnal mind of humanism, relativism. In reality, the church has been just as affected by the cultural side of humanism as the society we live in.

Only a "saltless" society can produce such a low level of morality, "and if the salt loses its savor, it is good for nothing but to be trampled underfoot by man." (Matthew 5:13 paraphrase)

In 2 Corinthians 11, Paul, speaking of the "different gospel," said that the Corinthians "tolerated" the different gospel, different Jesus, and different spirit. And the effect of that "tolerance" was to undermine their singleness of devotion to the Lord Jesus Christ. You *cannot* serve two masters.

When the absolute authority of the Word of God is compromised in the hearts and minds of His people, there is an extreme downward spiritual slide. Where there is no *absolute authority*, there can be no correction. And if I am without need of *correction*, because only what I think about the Word is what matters to me, Hebrews 12:8 states that I am "illegitimate offspring"—as the Amplified version politely puts it.

Of course, this is speaking of our spiritual relationship with the Father of Spirits. *If the sons of God are going to mature and step forth to manifest the righteous, legitimate authority of the Father in the earth, they will of necessity need to be "legitimate" sons, subject to correction, which the carnal mind is* not!

This will only come about as the "legitimate sons" *submit* themselves to the Father for correction, the crucifying of the flesh, training the senses, through living by faith from the realm of the Spirit.

In the United States, our politically correct culture, leaning more towards Humanism each day, will not *allow* or tolerate the concept of "correction." The only exception is if you are the "intellectually elite"— then you have the privilege of correcting humanity.

We must value and submit to the *Enlightening of the Word and the Spirit* and reject the influence of the "intellectually elite." If we are absorbed by the spirit of the world, we will be the "salt trampled underfoot" that is useless.

So let's first redeem and recover the value of "correction" and set it in context accurately with Hebrews 12:5-11. If you have seen the power of the carnal mind to sabotage the believer, you are probably in a good place to rejoice, knowing that our Father, through correction with the sword of the Spirit, the Word of God, will divide the flesh from the spirit and walk us out of this fog into the clear light of reality—the Truth.

If we don't think we need correction, we are saying we don't err (are never deceived.) As stated previously, if we don't think we can be deceived, we are deceived!

It is the "mind of the flesh" that does not subject itself to the Father. (Romans 8:7) In light of that reality, it seems to me that we would RUN to the Father to submit and receive teaching, training, and instruction.

If we can recover the value of authority and correction and learn how and why God corrects us, we will then be aligned to work with Him and submit to this aspect of our relationship with the Father of Spirits.

Obviously, as individual sons, whatever correction we go through will be unique in some way. Therefore, we will present principles from the Word that will renew our minds and value system.

But before we look into Hebrews 12, let's look at Isaiah 30:18, as I believe it reveals the Father's heart and motivation toward all mankind and specifically toward those who have become His own children.

"And therefore the Lord (earnestly) waits (expecting, looking and longing) to be gracious to you; and therefore He lifts Himself up, that He may have mercy on you and show lovingkindness to you. For the Lord is a God of justice. Blessed are all those who (earnestly) wait for Him, who expect and look and long for Him (for His victory, His favor, His love, His peace, His joy, and His matchless unbroken companionship!)" (Isaiah 30:18 AMP)

Particularly in the Old Testament, there is a clear and consistent portrayal of God's attitude toward mankind. Verses 15-17 of Isaiah 30 reference the nature of man to consistently rebel towards the Lord and do things his own way. But the statement of God's intense desire to lavish all of His goodness on mankind is made in Verse 18, almost in disregard to man's nature. He is waiting, even as the father waited for the prodigal son.

Speaking of His goodness, Exodus 33:19 (AMP) says, "For I will be gracious to whom I will be gracious, and will show mercy and lovingkindness on whom I will show mercy and lovingkindness."

I don't believe this is a statement of selection and predestination, but rather a statement of God's total disposition toward mankind, to "whosoever believeth."

The word *mercy* here means "yearning, longing to release and impart all His life, favor, kindness, goodness."

"The Lord delights in mercy" (Micah 7:18 AMP), meaning He is disposed to showing favor. He *desires* to do this. So even in correction, His heart motivation doesn't change. That's why Hebrews 12 states it's for our "certain (absolute) good."

Two words used in Hebrews 12 are "chasten" and "scourge." *Chasten* means "to teach, train, instruct." *Scourge* means "blow, whip."

There are commentaries that state God afflicts us with evil and calamity to chasten (teach) and scourge. We have to interpret "scourge" here in terms of words, not literal in any way. We know that Jesus was "scourged" for our sins, so there is no legal or spiritual validity to this being literal scourging. He is called the "Father of Spirits" in this passage on correction.

Since one of the main ways to interpret the Word is based on the character and nature of God, I cannot embrace interpretations that picture God afflicting His children with evil and calamity. Neither has my considerable life experience as a believer been that God sends evil and calamity to teach me, any more than I send evil and calamity to teach *my* children. However, I can testify to the need and value of the seasons of correction! *smile*

In the natural, most evil and calamity comes upon our children from their refusal of correction and wisdom, while we stand by and pray for God's mercy in the midst of those circumstances. Likewise, I believe that we mostly bring those circumstances upon ourselves for the same reasons.

"My people are destroyed for lack of knowledge." (Hosea 4:6 KJV) Wouldn't we be fools to refuse personal mentoring when the Word says that without it, we will be destroyed?

One will need to settle two issues before Hebrews 12 can be for one's good. Firstly, that God is not sending calamity to correct you, but He will help you (through correction) to recover from calamity. Secondly, that correction is, indeed, valuable and good!

What to look for in Hebrews 12:5-11—

- God is dealing with you as *sons*, not servants who have no inheritance. The son must mature before being able to administrate his inheritance. Maturing comes as we submit to His correction, in which the Word of God will always be present.

- The Father corrects every son whom He loves. This is a good time to point out that John 14:21-24 states three times that *our love* for the Father is known by our obedience to Him, without which there would be no correction. This may be fairly new revelation to some: Father God *corrects* whom He *loves*, and legitimate sons that love the Father *submit* to and *obey* Him. That portion of John 14 also reveals incredible promises of presence and revelation related to obedience to Him. "I will come to him and make My abode with him"—speaking of the one who obeys.

- This correction is for our "CERTAIN (absolute) GOOD." Let's renew our minds from the humanism of the day. Correction (teaching, training and instruction from the Father) is *good!*

- We are exhorted "don't despise"—look down upon, detest, or take lightly—this correction. Hmmm. I'm thinking that means we need to repent—do a 180—because detesting is mostly our mindset towards correction.

Lord, we pause now to remove the obstacle that hinders our benefitting from Your mercy and goodness offered to us in the form of "correction." We repent and cast down the imagination of the flesh that would take us captive and prevent our experiencing the glorious freedom of the sons of God. We confess this attitude as sin and choose to turn from it. We actively and violently pull down all the humanistic thinking that surrounds the lies about correction—we release all experiences and people connected to the lie about authority and correction. We bring every thought into captivity to *obey* Christ.

We declare that our negative thinking about correction and authority is a lie—and the Truth is the Father of Spirits, our Heavenly Father, corrects us because He dearly loves us and all that He does for us is for our *certain good.* So now we move into thanking You for this *provision* to help mature us and conform us to Your image.

We also thank You for forgiving us and cleansing us from this unrighteousness, and we receive release from this iniquity.

- We must "submit" (subject, come under, lower, humble) to correction if we want to be "Fathered." We will never be free from the "orphan" spirit (rejection) without submitting to the Father.
- "For the time, no correction is pleasant." There will be some pain, for gain. God doesn't put sickness on us, but we can learn and be corrected in sickness. God doesn't put emotional or mental pain upon us, but in the midst of those pains, we can turn to Him and be corrected and delivered... and mature.

I have found that the greatest pain of correction was to realize what damage I have done to others and what loss may have been incurred for others through me or because of me. That is truly painful and can cause much regret. Thankfully, we can release and recover from that pain.

- The Father of Spirits uses His Word, Truth, implemented by Holy Spirit, to accomplish everything. He teaches, trains and instructs by His Word. Failure to heed and obey His Word will bring us into situations that will need correction. If we are wiser than King Asa, we will not get angry but will repent when needed correction comes from Him. By the way, submitting to Father God delivers us out of the hands of demons and man, so whose hands would you rather be in?

- Lastly, the result of the correction is "peaceable fruit of righteousness."

"The effect of righteousness is peace." (Isaiah 32:17)

If we remember Hebrews 5:13-14, about maturing, becoming skilled in the word of righteousness, having our senses exercised to discern good and evil, it will increase our appreciation of this awesome opportunity to be mentored by the Father of Spirits, who is also the Father of Lights, from whom every good and perfect thing comes down. (James 1:17)

Finally, Hebrews 12:11-13 reveals the deep empathy of the Father and offers comfort in the process that He says "seems grievous and painful." The exhortation is that in the midst of what is, *in our human experience*, grievous and painful, we recognize this effect on one's personality and move in faith, that the "weakened, drooping hands and feet may be cured"—and not entirely put out of joint, which is a worse condition.

Isaiah 61 says to *put on* the garment of praise to replace the spirit of heaviness—lift up your voice to God. Take the oil of joy for the spirit of mourning. In other words, during this process (some are longer and more painful than others), by faith, appropriate and stir up the joy which belongs to you, to ensure that your experience is beneficial, not bitter!

17

GHOSTS OF THE PAST

O Lord, Our God, other masters besides You have ruled over us, but we will ACKNOWLEDGE and mention your name only. They (former tyrant masters) are dead, they shall not live and reappear; they are *powerless ghosts*, they shall not rise and come back. Therefore, You have visited and made an end of them and caused every memory of them to perish." (Isaiah 16:13-14 AMP)

In Christ—if and as we walk by faith in the New Creation Reality—every memory of the past masters will perish. This isn't speaking only of exercising "authority and power" as we do over sickness and disease, but the power of *living* in the New Creation.

These ghosts are part of the snare spoken of in 2 Timothy 2:25-26, recovering ourselves, being delivered from regret and remorse forever by *acknowledging* the truth—we will *acknowledge* ONLY YOU.

Remorse and regret means "looking back and wishing—knowing that you *could* have—thinking that you *should* have—why didn't you...?" It is actually the carnal mind harassing and tormenting you with memories that we haven't allowed the blood of Jesus to blot out.

Matthew 27 in the KJV says Judas "repented himself." But if you look at his actions and the outcome, you realize it isn't Bible repentance, but what is called "remorse."

Remorse means to be afflicted in the mind and troubled about former folly. Judas tried to clear his conscience and pay penance by returning the thirty pieces of silver. He was trying to rid himself of that inner nagging.

Regret and remorse are powerful "ghosts" to a believer. We feel we can justify pre-salvation behavior—but it's those things that we do and experience *after salvation* that are the ghosts that eat away at the reality of the New Creation.

The example of Judas can clarify and bring us to an awareness of a weakness that we need to see, repent of, and "deliver ourselves" from. Disappointment with ourselves leads to despair and some degree of depression, becoming somewhat hopeless, lifeless, unmotivated. And it sets up the "pendulum effect," feeling like a ping pong ball, back and forth. It is the "buffeting" of shame and pride. "Pride cometh, shame cometh." (Proverbs 11:2)

My husband, while seeking counsel from one of his favorite, wise Bible school teachers, asked, "Why do I have so much trouble forgiving myself?" To which the teacher responded very simply, "It is pride." I guess this is saying the hardest person to forgive is *yourself*. But that also reveals that we are allowing the carnal mind to occupy space in our conscience—the inner man that Hebrews tells us is cleansed by the blood of Jesus, "once for all."

Paul speaks of a "messenger from satan" sent to "buffet" him, meaning to "torment and torture." (2 Corinthians 12) It is a good possibility that he was referring to exactly what we are talking about: regret, remorse, over his past. He was totally wrong (as Saul), but he thought he was totally right! He was a Jew among Jews!

How do we know that Paul, with the grace (operational ability) of God, was able to overcome and disarm the ghosts of his past, the blood of Christians on his hands?

"Therefore since these great promises are ours, beloved, let us cleanse ourselves from everything that contaminates and defiles body and spirit [do the ghosts of regret and remorse defile?] and bring our consecration to completeness in the fear of God." (2 Corinthians 7:1 AMP—author emphasis added)

Verse 2 says, "Do open your hearts to us again. We have wronged no one." This could have stirred up all kinds of thoughts, feelings, animosity for those listening to Paul. The audacity of him making this statement. I'm sure some thought he should be punished forever for all the Christians that he was responsible for slaughtering.

We see a stark contrast between Paul—who learned, understood, and lived by the power of the Spirit—and Judas who lived by the power of flesh. The carnal mind has *no* power over the ghosts, as seen with Judas. In fact, the carnal mind is driven by the "pride of life"—so it cannot deliver itself... from itself!

Again, we see the defining line between the life of the flesh (good and bad) and the life of the spirit. It is "reliance." What power are you *relying* upon to deal with the ghosts, in a way that they are rendered "powerless"?

How did Paul overcome this "buffeting" in contrast to Judas? Paul could have said, "I will just kill myself because I can't escape the pain, torment, torture of the ghosts." The key is found in 2 Corinthians 12: the grace (operational ability, power of the spirit) is sufficient, meaning, "more than enough."

The enemy has been stripped of actual power, having only the power of lies, suggestions and accusations. As we have seen, the "pride of life" is an effective tool in his arsenal of accusations.

The believer, who learns to *believe* and live from the New Creation Realities spoken of in 2 Corinthians 5, can truly experience a life in which even the "memory" of those ghosts is blotted out!

"I thank God, whom I worship with a clear conscience." (2 Timothy 1:3)

Paul, who brought the revelation in Hebrews 9 and 10 of a purified conscience, was living this revelation. The Word emphatically states in Hebrews 1:3 (AMP) that when Christ had by offering Himself accomplished our cleansing of sin *and riddance of guilt* (conscience), sat down at the right hand of the divine Majesty on high.

Notice, it isn't *just* cleansing of sin, but cleansing of the consciousness of sin, riddance of guilt. Also, Hebrews 9:14 (10:22 and others AMP), "How much more shall the blood of Christ *purge* (cleanse) our consciences from dead works and lifeless observances to serve the Living God?" This is the capstone of the finished work of Christ... and He sat down...

"Now where remission (to be remitted) of these (sins) is, there is no more offering for sin." (Hebrews 10:18 KJV paraphrase) To "remit" is to cancel the penalty, as though there was no transgression. In this way, God addressed the penalty mankind was bearing as a result of Adam's fall, spiritual death. This has been done—"once and for all."

Seriously, Pastor Alyce... are you saying the memories, the ghosts, have REALLY been BLOTTED OUT? Yes, seriously, personally, and experientially, as surely as my sins have been blotted out!!

But because we are still subjected to the powers of darkness on earth, God gives us 1 John 1:9... based on the present High Priestly ministry of Jesus Christ.

"If we confess our sins, He is faithful and just to forgive us our sins, and to cleanse us from *all* unrighteousness." (1 John 1:9 KJV)

The neglect of *authentic faith* teaching has rendered these and other scriptures mere head knowledge, to which we give mental assent. It is the justification, received by faith, the righteousness which is of faith, the cleansed conscience which is appropriated through faith, that are the bedrock of the New Creation Realities taught and lived by the Apostle Paul. But if the foundation of faith is neglected, we have no recourse but to live by sense knowledge, feelings, experiences, and the carnal mind.

God's ultimate purpose for every born again believer is to live and walk in the awareness of the "New Creation," transformed, living in a way that eliminates a dwelling place for ghosts of the past to hide and haunt. His stated will: the memory of past masters blotted out!

18

The Spirit of Amalek

Let's take this a little further. "And the Lord said to Moses—Write this for a memorial in the book—rehearse it in the ears of Joshua... that I will utterly blot out the remembrance of Amalek from under the heavens... because theirs is a hand against the throne of the Lord— the Lord will have war with Amalek from generation to generation." (Exodus 17:14,16 AMP) "Throne of the Lord" is a reference to the Sovereignty of God.

We have all heard a lot about the "-ites" in the Old Testament, but we need to understand the significance of Amalek and the Amalekites. It will help deliver us from the ghosts.

Isaac was the son of promise (spirit); and Ishmael, his half-brother, was the son of flesh. Ishmael hated and persecuted Isaac. The Book of Genesis also tells us the same about Esau and his brother Jacob. Esau hated Jacob. Clearly, Esau, who despised his birthright and traded it for a bowl of pottage, was the son of flesh, and Jacob, later renamed Israel, was the son of promise (spirit.)

As Galatians 4 states, that which is of the flesh always persecutes that which is of the spirit. What does this have to do with Amalek? He was the *grandson* of Esau and obviously carried the same spirit. Amalek represents the whole realm of the natural man (humanism) that persecutes that which is born of the spirit.

Based on the scriptural record of statements by God regarding Amalek, and the activities of Amalek, he possessed the hatred that was in Esau, particularly regarding the birthright that he lost. As the scripture states, the Lord will have war with Amalek (carnal mind of man) from generation to generation. The scripture says Amalek is a "hand against the throne (sovereignty) of God." Recall the statement of Lucifer: "I will exalt my throne *above* the stars of God." (Isaiah 14:13 AMP)

So this enemy seems to embody something more than the other enemies of God's people in the Old Testament. Like Secular Humanism today, it seems to be of a more complete nature. The name "Amalek" literally means, "One who devours what is around him." It also means "to cut the neck—sever the head"—that is, make a Headless Body.

Amalek was a real person. The Word says specific things about "this enemy" that are relevant and helpful to us and, at the same time, issue a strong warning.

As a significant example of a "hand against the throne of God," we see that Amalek was the first nation to attack the children of Israel as they were being delivered from Egypt. And God took note:

"Remember what Amalek did to you on the way when you had come forth from Egypt. But when you were faint and weary, attacked you along the way. Therefore, *when* the Lord your God has given you *rest* from all your enemies round about in the land which the Lord your God gives you to possess as an inheritance (the Natural Promised Land), *you shall blot out the remembrance of Amalek from under the heavens. You must not forget!*" (Deuteronomy 25:17-19 AMP, emphasis added)

Amalek had no fear of God and His demonstrated sovereignty by miracles to deliver His people from Egypt. This is a very clear word to the church today. We all understand that the "natural deliverance," including the blood of the lamb on the doorposts, is a picture of our spiritual salvation, being delivered and translated out of darkness into the Kingdom of His Dear Son.

We also know that the Promised Rest in the land they would possess is a picture of the *rest* spoken of in Hebrews 4, the New Creation Reality. I believe the words, "You shall blot out the remembrance of Amalek from under the heavens. You must not forget!" is as directive and relevant to the church today as it was to Joshua.

When Joshua led the children of Israel into the Promised Land, they did, indeed, *temporarily* blot out Amalek. But the Word says that after Joshua died, the next generation didn't fear God, didn't know the Lord or His works on behalf of Israel. And, years later, an alliance that included Amalek took back Jericho.

The spirit of Amalek is very active today. It is set on world dominion and world destruction. It is a religious war, in the spirit and the natural.

More serious is the spirit of Amalek over the arising Body of Christ through the activity of the carnal mind, with the intent of neutralizing on earth, so as to "devour," the only real obstacle to the spirit of Amalek, the living Body of Christ with its Head, Jesus Christ.

If the parallels of the deliverance from Egypt and entrance into the Promised Land represent our spiritual deliverance and Promised Land, then surely the order to "blot out" the remembrance of Amalek in the land we possess is for us, too. We need to see that Amalek was not the "run of the mill" enemy of God.

One more well-known event adds emphasis to the significance of Amalek. "Samuel also said unto Saul, the Lord sent me to anoint thee to be king over his people, over Israel; now therefore hearken thou unto the voice of the words of the Lord. Thus saith the Lord of hosts, I *remember* that which Amalek did to Israel, how he laid wait for him in the way, when he came up from Egypt. Now go and smite Amalek and utterly destroy all that they have and spare them not." (2 Samuel 15:1-2 AMP)

With the understanding of Amalek and all that this spirit represents, the events of this passage are more impacting. Going on, you can read the following scriptures, but you probably know the story. When Saul was confronted by Samuel, he said, "I have obeyed, but the people have done this." (Verse 20) But he hadn't obeyed, so Samuel says, "Because you have rejected the word of the Lord, He also has rejected you from being king." (Verse 23) Saul realizes, "...Because I feared the people and obeyed their voice." (Verse 24) He didn't fear the Lord and destroy Amalek... he feared the people, he identified with the people—rather than God.

Could this be insight, a warning, as to why the church today has been so weak and compromised, not possessing the land of promise of the Spirit... because we haven't destroyed Amalek in our own territory, our own lives? And it was because we feared the people more than we feared God?

"Bring here to me Agag, king of the Amalekites, and Samuel hewed Agag in pieces before the Lord in Gilgal." (Verse 32) "You have rejected the word of the Lord, and the Lord hath rejected you as king."

A few things we must point out: God said, "Blot out Amalek and the remembrance of Amalek." The carnal mind. If we are to "possess the land" of the New Creation Reality, we *must* not allow the spirit of

Amalek any place, any opportunity. We must *acknowledge only* our God, our Savior, our Deliverer.

If we don't "cut off" Amalek, that spirit will cut us off from the Head. It will devour all to which it is given access. The spirit of Amalek is a hand against God, from generation to generation, and God said we must not forget!

19

ADVANCE!

One Sunday morning a few months ago, I was finishing my time meditating on the morning message, and I heard the Lord say, "ADVANCE!" Being really short on time, I checked Bible Gateway quickly; and the first thing that popped up, from a preset translation, not one of my choosing, was from Joshua 6:7, "And he said to the army, *Advance!*"

This was a significant prophetic word to us because of what we had been studying. The word *advance* means "move forward with purpose." Not that we have to wait for a word; this is always a word to the Body of Christ: **Advance!**

The scripture passage was the entering of the Promised Land and taking of Jericho led by Joshua. What can we take spiritually from the directive God gave Joshua and the children of Israel about entering the natural Promised Land?

"Now Jericho (a fenced city with high walls) was tightly closed because of the Israelites; no one went out or came in. (It was impenetrable.) And the Lord said to Joshua, *See*, I have given Jericho, its king and mighty men of valor, into your hands. You shall march around the enclosure, all your men of war going around the city..." (Joshua 6:1-2 paraphrase)

If you noticed, first God said to Joshua, "*Look* at this impossible situation—**then,** *listen* to how *we* are going to do the impossible... together!"

It is apparent that Joshua had to totally *rely* on God and His provision, and the army had to totally *rely* on Joshua, as he *relied* on God. Even though the Word says this was an army—armed men—they did *not* use those natural weapons to take this IMPENETRABLE STRONGHOLD. God *could* have given them victory through a natural battle with natural weapons, but I believe it is the living application of "not carnal weapons" that also shows us the way into *our Promised Land.*

Faith. What a simple word—but what profound power is released to the one who "digs down deep" and acts, in faith, upon the Word of God, our Source of Faith.

So let's see what we can do to perhaps sharpen our sword, the Word of God, so that all we have spoken of in this book can become reality, not just theory.

I want to share a few basics that I believe get lost in the labyrinth of mental assent, which by the way, is a work of the carnal mind: hearing the Word, nodding agreement, but not acting upon the Word.

At one point in our life (my husband and I), we had both become really desperate for change. We weren't bad. In fact, we were good! Regular church attendance, tithers, workers, singers, youth leaders, etc. You name it, we did it! We were actually considered *leaders.*

But one day we looked around and said, "Uh, if *we* are the leaders, we are in TROUBLE!" So we began to seek God—we had no idea of how to move from where we were to more of God. I won't go into the long version of that story right now, but God heard and answered, and we made some major moves in our life which changed us forever! God was saying to us, "Advance!"

These "moves" were *not* confirmed or agreed upon by our leaders (with whom we did consult) or our families; but we had heard God, and He had confirmed with signs and miracles of provision. So we started on a journey to a "place that we knew not" kinda like Abraham. It was *definitely* a faith journey. And when I say move, we literally left one part of the United States and moved to another part... away.

God did miracles of provision to get us from point A to point B, so we thought we were really strong faith giants, really had a handle on this "faith"—until we got to point B. And at that place, we had to learn what it means to "live and walk by faith"—not just have God do miracles of provision to move you!

We started meeting with a small group in a small store-front building that had some grasp of the Word—and faith—that we didn't have. So as we listened to their testimonies, we said, "Oh, we can do that." So we tried—and we failed...and we were frustrated. "Why isn't this working for me?"

Oh, you've said that, too?

So when we calmed down and really got in a place where God could show us the problem, we began to understand that testimonies are great—and are prophetic—but it still requires the Word of God living in your heart, as it was in *their heart*, to bring forth fruit of faith.

We are eternally thankful for the great faith leaders of our time—and of earlier generations. But sometimes we depend more upon "faith teaching" than upon the *Word* that teaches faith.

There have been times that I have felt very confused about certain faith testimonies and certain faith teaching. But the Teacher of the church, Holy Spirit, has always led me back to the solid, unchangeable, infallible Word of God. It endures forever!

Faith is really simple. But when we don't recognize the enemy of God, the carnal mind (Romans 8:7), it becomes complicated. Man's senses, if untrained in the Word of Righteousness, will always work *with* the logic and reasonings of the carnal mind, *against* the Mind of Christ, the Mind of the Spirit...and Faith.

The carnal mind is referred to as the "understanding" that we are to "lean not" upon. (Proverbs 3:5-6) If we trust in the Lord with all our heart, we can have the peace of God that "surpasses understanding," that will "keep (guard) your heart and mind in Christ Jesus." (Philippians 4:7)

Here's a tip: *You need this peace!* And the carnal mind cannot give peace, nor will it allow you to live in peace. The carnal mind is the antithesis of faith and peace.

20

DEFINING FAITH

S o I want to offer a few basic explanations and definitions of faith that we have gained in our forty-plus years of journey and will continue living by as long as we are on earth. I believe they will be helpful to you. We will clarify the following:

- What is it to "believe" in the way the Bible speaks of believing?
- What defines faith—and separates it from believing?
- What is mental assent?
- What is unbelief?
- What about "receiving" by faith, claiming, appropriating?
- What is denial?
- What is presumption?

We are offering our definition of faith, which incorporates all the above concepts. Faith is to be influenced, fully persuaded, and won over to the superiority of the Kingdom of God and the Word of that Kingdom.

1. *Believe* means to be "fully persuaded"—a persuasion that leads to "unqualified committal to and reliance upon."

Immediately we must know we are *not* talking about the MIND being fully persuaded, but the HEART, the inner man. At first, *no one's mind is persuaded.*

"Because if you acknowledge (confess) with your lips (audibly) that Jesus is Lord and believe in your heart that God raised Him from the dead, you will be saved. For with the heart man believeth unto righteousness and with the mouth confession is made unto salvation." (Romans 10: 9-10 AMP)

These scriptures contain the basic principle of faith, as it is talking about our initial encounter of faith—that is, salvation. All other *faith* is based upon the same faith principle, "believing in your heart" and "acknowledging with your mouth."

> 2. Defining faith. Faith is action taken in life—responding in life to the "believing in your heart." We all *live* what we *believe.*

Unfortunately, many of us do not know what is in our heart because of the subliminal effect. But Jesus taught that a man's heart is known by specific criteria, which is important because the Word teaches that *we* cannot actually know our own heart. We won't take time to develop that thought, but we will just accept it as truth. Here's how the Word judges: "For as he thinks in his heart, so is he." (Proverbs 23:7 AMP) "Out of the fullness (the overflow, the superabundance) of the heart, the mouth speaks." (Matthew 12:34 AMP)

Matthew 15 and Mark 7 show it is what comes out of the heart, thoughts and actions, that defile a man.

"What you treasure the most—reveals your heart." (Matthew 6:21)

"For everyone who comes to Me and listens to My words and *does* them, I will show you what he is like. He is like a man building a house, who dug and went down deep and laid a foundation upon the rock." (Luke 6:47-48 AMP) Remember, this is Jesus speaking, *the* Rock.

We all "believe" something in our heart. Acting upon that "believing" is called FAITH, if it is in response to the Word of God.

Our FAITH will only be as strong as the inner persuasion (believing) of the Living Word... in our heart. It is futile to think that "acting on the Word"—without being fully persuaded in your heart, will produce fruit. IF your heart isn't fully persuaded by the Word in a particular situation—but you try to act upon the Word in that situation, it will only be fulfilling the scripture in James 1:7-8... "a double-minded man is unstable in all his ways"... and let not that man think he will receive anything from the Lord. We are talking about "believing in the heart—and acting upon what you believe, what you are persuaded of, in the heart." Now that you know about the carnal mind, you can recognize the enemy that opposes your faith—and cast down the imaginations that arise when you act on the Word that you are persuaded of.

- Faith has corresponding actions based on the Word of God.
- Faith without corresponding actions is called "dead." (James 2:26)
- Faith acts upon the Word of God, which is Revelation Knowledge, in contrast to "knowledge" based upon sense, reason, feeling, circumstance.

3. What is mental assent? I call mental assent a counterfeit, an imitation. It is also referred to as "head knowledge."

If you start with the definitions of "believe" and "faith," then mental assent will not be as confusing. Banks have had a practice of training tellers to recognize *counterfeit* money by only allowing them to handle the real money. Their *sense of touch* becomes trained, and they can recognize counterfeit money in that way.

Mental assent is much the same. It is the doublemindedness spoken of in James 1. It is having a knowledge of scripture, perhaps even quoting the scripture, agreeing with the scripture (meaning it doesn't *disagree*), saying the scripture is true... *but does not rely and act upon it.*

Repeating, if you put the definitions of "believe" and "faith" into practice, you will be well on your way to recognizing "mental assent." Mental Assent isn't *really* fully persuaded in the heart, with unqualified committal. It does not *act* upon the Word... but it talks about the Word. The TALK of mental assent can be much the same as a believer, but the WALK of mental assent cannot—it is very different! Mark 4, verses 16 & 17, speaks of the Word not becoming rooted in the heart; therefore, it is easily "uprooted" by trouble and persecution.

4. What is unbelief? One definition offered is "to be unable to believe as result of not having a strong enough belief system in place (in the heart)." That might mean one who has not become "fully persuaded."

Unbelief, like mental assent, does not act upon the Word. It may not be as deceiving as mental assent—it may be more honest, but unbelief and mental assent are very similar.

E.W. Kenyon offers this insight about unbelief: There are two kinds of unbelief:

a. Lack of Knowledge of the Word (in your heart). Not being grounded enough in the Word to act in faith. This is very similar to what is stated above.

b. Unpersuadableness. This unbelief is a matter of will. Believing is a choice, an act of the will. He can act on the Word—if he will.

We know to believe is to be persuaded. So believing is aligning your will with His Will (His Word.) An unpersuadable attitude toward the Word of God is a man that is unwilling to allow the Word of God to *govern* him. Hence the similarity of Mental Assent and Unbelief. There must be a willingness to embrace the "whole counsel of God"— without splicing and dicing, picking your favorite scriptures.

Mental Assent will be *dismantled* if you acknowledge the sin of unbelief. (John 16:9)

5. Receiving by faith. A few scriptures give us the basis of this principle. Hebrews 11 is known as the "faith chapter" in the Bible, and rightly so.

"Now faith is..." (Hebrews 11:1) If you have been confused because of the reference to "faith is now," perhaps I can clarify that. As you can see, the word "faith" is sandwiched between two present tense words, NOW and IS.

The reason for that is because "faith" is not of the natural, time-bound world in which we live. Rather, it is of the eternal realm. Faith is of the unseen, invisible realm, the realm of *no time*. Faith is not subject to, governed by, TIME. So it is always "now." Of course, that goes for the Word of God also...it is of the eternal, "now" realm.

Hebrews goes on to say that the world we see, *that is visible*, was made from that which is *invisible, by the words (of faith) that God spoke.*

So when authentic Bible faith is in operation, the same is happening. The eternal "now" of faith is reaching into and bringing the invisible into the visible.

That doesn't mean you will see the invisible manifest in the visible realm at that exact *time*, but you *will* see it. (Often, especially when praying for others, we *do* see a manifestation into the visible realm at that time.)

Second Corinthians 4:18 (paraphrase) speaks of the spirit of faith and says that "while we *look not* (focus, center on) at the things that are seen, but at the unseen. For the things that are seen (with natural eyes) are temporal, subject to change, but the things that are unseen are unchangeable, eternal."

A couple more things on receiving. Jesus said in Mark 11, "When you pray, believe you receive." Many things have been said about this scripture, but I will offer what I have come to understand. If you use the original definition of "believe" (fully persuaded, unqualified committal) then *receiving comes with the believing.* And Jesus is saying— believe it, because it is true--rather than *try* to believe you are receiving.

Obviously, Jesus is talking about faith and the invisible reality, not that what you prayed for is always immediately in your physical possession at the time. When God is speaking of faith and the Spirit, we must think in terms of faith and the Spirit, lest we err. Faith looks at the unseen and receives what God has promised—before it is seen.

What do I base that upon? The words of Jesus, "I assure you, most solemnly I tell you, he who *believes* in Me, *has* [**now possesses**] eternal life." (John 6:47 AMP) This scripture declares believing is receiving, *now* possessing.

Do we question that statement? No. We believe when we confess Jesus as our Savior that we *do indeed* receive eternal life. The basic act of faith is the foundation of our salvation and the basic faith principle of all other promises of God. We don't doubt that heaven is our eternal home, even though an angel didn't show up with a heavenly deed, proving our possession... or even to congratulate us!! We believe!

John 1:12 (KJV) also seems to support this principle of receiving: "But as many as *received Him, to them* gave He power to *become* the Sons of God, even to them that *believe on his name:*"

The "receiving" came at the time of "believing." And Jesus says in Mark 11, "Believe you have received—because you have!" But if you don't believe it, you think you are still trying to "get" something from God. That which you have received from the spirit realm when you prayed, you could say was deposited in your account, will never become reality. Why? Because of *unbelief.* Believing that you *did* receive when you prayed is "appropriating, claiming" the gift given.

When you are born again, a literal "kingdom" doesn't fall out of heaven into your yard! But you believe you received eternal life without sight, regardless of feeling.

Most people leave it there, thinking they shouldn't touch Eternal Life until they go to heaven. Maybe they need to "save up" or something. (I am being facetious.)

At the New Birth, a believer possesses *all* that the Bible says they are heir to, as joint heirs with Jesus. And you have access into this grace by **faith**!

6. What is denial? Denial in psychology (study of the mind) is called a defense mechanism against external realities that threaten the ego. Depending on the person, it can be an almost subconscious defense in the mind when one is unable to find a way to come to terms with what they are experiencing in natural life.

It is important to realize this is a "natural" activity of the carnal, sense-ruled mind. So that means it will *benefit nothing* in terms of actually resolving issues in life, as the source of its operation (flesh) actually *denies* the power of God in any given situation. Denial is very close to the metaphysical "mind over matter" practice, which originates in the carnal mind, not the believing heart. It will leave the believer in a worse situation when it doesn't bring fruit, as it causes confusion and disappointment.

Sometimes denial in a believer is a perversion or misunderstanding of the scripture in Romans 4:17 which says, "God calls the things that be not, as though they were."

But denial calls the things that "be" as though they "be not." The *reasonings* of the carnal mind assume it is the same, but it isn't. One is faith (God's way)—the other is denial (man's way.)

People often confuse the act of "denying" the natural reality of a situation with acting in faith. Authentic faith does *not* deny the existence or natural reality of anything. Authentic faith is the most powerful and freeing manner in which to address the issues we all experience in earthlife.

Only as you acknowledge a need, loss, fear, etc., can you then "acknowledge" that you do not have, in yourself, the personal resources to change or rise above a situation. Acknowledging your need and calling on the Name of the Lord will bring His presence, power and authority to bear upon the issues. "You shall know the truth, and the truth shall make you free." (John 8:32 KJV)

7. What about presumption? From the New Testament, and being similar to the Old Testament use, the word presumption means "to be daring, to be without fear or dread in relationship with God."

"Let Him be your fear and let Him be your dread lest you offend Him by your fear of man and distrust of Him." (Isaiah 8:13 AMP) The Bible definition of presumption is much more serious than our contemporary, indifferent definition. It carries the thought of being "self-assured, confident in one's own thoughts and resources," in disregard to the written Word of God. The Old Testament speaks of a man "not listening" to the word of the Lord and also states that when they fear the Lord, they will not act presumptuously again.

It is also important to note that presumption is fruit of pride. The word "blinded" in 2 Corinthians 4:4 can also be translated "smokescreen." Blinded is closely connected to the root word for pride in the New Testament.

Taken altogether, I think this attitude, presumption, should be viewed with "fear and dread." We must exercise great caution in our faith walk to humble ourselves before the Word and Spirit of God, making sure that we don't enter into another strong counterfeit of faith—presumption, being self-confident, self-assured, while quoting the promises of God.

Usually by the time you discover, by experience, that you have been blinded, great damage has been done. And since pride is the root of presumption, and pride does not humble itself before the Lord, this would be one of those very serious snares in which we must recover ourselves by repentance and acknowledging the truth according to 2 Timothy 2:25-26 KJV.

21

THE CONFESSION OF FAITH

What we have gained from years of the faith walk, with our victories and failures, joy and tears, is the importance of what Paul talked about in 2 Corinthians 11:1-4. He speaks of being seduced away from the simplicity of devotion to Jesus Christ. And everything that draws us is called "the other or different gospel." We have looked at that "different gospel" and seen that it is the self-centered, people-centered, people-first gospel. The carnal mind is the driver behind that gospel.

Our considered opinion is that if one devotes himself, and continues to devote himself, to the Lord Jesus Christ, he will avoid many of the snares and counterfeits of faith that we have cautioned, even warned about, in this section on faith. And that is the simplicity of faith, devotion to, in covenant with the One to whom we are betrothed, Jesus Christ.

So let me wrap this up with one more *very* important principle of faith. You can call it confession, and that will be correct, as Jesus *is* the High Priest of our Confession. But I want to emphasize it as "acknowledging" (audibly, verbally.)

To "acknowledge" is to audibly speak what God says... who He is, what He does and will do, and who He has made you to be. We don't often think of that as praise, but that is exactly what it is.

This is better known as the "confession of faith"—again, as in salvation. *Faith speaks.* You can see it all through the New Testament.

What does faith say? It says what God says, in the spirit of faith, and that is why we must believe and put the Word into our heart, so we may act upon that Word (faith.) One of the primary actions is that we speak, acknowledge God, what He has done for us, who He has made us to be.

Check out these scriptures:

"Oh Lord, our God, other *masters* besides you have ruled over us, but we will *acknowledge and mention Your name only.*" (Isaiah 26: 13 AMP)

We could stop there! What a statement of faith! But there is more.

"Your faith becomes effectual by the *acknowledging of every good thing you have in Christ.*" (Philemon 6 paraphrase)

Another wow! "Effectual" means "working in power."

"In meekness instructing those that *oppose themselves*: if God peradventure will give them repentance to the *acknowledging of the truth*; and that they (who oppose themselves) may *recover themselves* out of the snare of the devil, who are taken captive by him at his will." (2 Timothy 2:25-26 paraphrase)

We know the devil is defeated and has no power to take us "captive at his will." The thought here is that when we don't *acknowledge the truth*, we are then vulnerable to this captivity (oppose themselves)—and can only deliver ourselves by the repentance of *acknowledging the truth.* That sounds a lot like becoming "persuaded" to align our will with the will of God, His Word.

Paul, recorded in the fourth chapter of Philippians, said he had found the "secret" (AMP)—to everything, every circumstance. I like to join that scripture with another scripture in 1 Thessalonians 5:18

(KJV)... "In everything give thanks, for this is the will of God in Christ Jesus concerning you."

There is no more powerful way to "acknowledge God"—than through thanksgiving. The practice of lifting your heart, lifting your hands, lifting your head, and lifting your voice to the Lord—acknowledging Him for Who He is, What He has Done, What He is Doing—works to activate and insulate your faith. This acknowledging, confessing and thanking God acts as a fortress against the carnal mind, as you wait patiently for the fulfillment of His Word.

"Trust in the Lord with all your heart; and do not rely on your own understanding. *In all thy ways acknowledge Him, and He shall direct thy paths.* Do not be wise in your own eyes; fear the Lord and depart from evil." (Proverbs 3:5-7 NKJV)

We *advance* into the Promised Land of the New Creation by faith. A wonderful exercise and action of that faith is "ACKNOWLEDGE and mention Your Name only."

22

THE ADVENTURE OF FAITH

We have never regretted our faith journey. We would not have traded our lives or lived our lives without God for any other life, regardless of whose life that is. There is no higher privilege than to be a son of God, living in relationship with Father God, living the adventure of faith on earth. And there is no greater inheritance one may leave on earth for family, friends and the Body of Christ.

In the Old Covenant, they were always looking forward, based on "promise." However, in the New Testament, the word "promise" doesn't carry the thought of something in the future. It carries the thought of "a *gift given* from God." A promise is an announcement of something that has already been provided by God, but can only be accessed by faith.

"For it is by grace that you are saved, through your faith." (Ephesians 2:8 AMP)

"Therefore inheriting the promise is the outcome of faith, in order that it might be given as an act of grace...." (Romans 4:16 AMP)

"Through Him we have access by faith, into this grace, in which we stand." (Romans 5:2 AMP)

All of the powerful teachings of grace, of all that God has done for us, will be deferred to a time when we leave this earth, if authentic faith isn't taught alongside of grace. If we fail to realize and act upon the access we have, through faith, to the New Creation, we will have no choice but to struggle with the carnal nature and the carnal mind while on earth.

Too many scriptures speak of the "now" of faith, God's will on earth as demonstrated through the First Adam, the Book of Acts, and the Last Adam, to convince me to defer this inheritance till I depart this house of flesh. You will find that theme throughout the Word of God.

"The heavens are the Lord's heavens, but the earth has He given to the children of men." (Psalm 115:16 AMP)

"The spirit of the Lord is upon Me, because He has anointed Me to preach the good news to the poor. He has sent me to announce release to the captives and recovery of sight to the blind, *to send forth AS DELIVERED those who are oppressed, to proclaim the accepted and acceptable year of the Lord, when salvation and the free favors of God profusely abound.*" (Luke 4:18 AMP)

"Let us therefore be zealous and exert ourselves and strive diligently to enter that rest (of God, to know and experience it for ourselves), that no one may fall or perish by the same kind of unbelief and disobedience (into which those in the wilderness fell). For the Word that God speaks is alive and full of power; it is sharper than any two-edged sword, penetrating to the dividing line of the breath of life (soul) and the spirit, and of joints and marrow, exposing and sifting and analyzing and judging the very thoughts and purposes of the heart." (Hebrews 4:11-12 AMP)

Notes

Notes

Notes